W9-CCQ-135

GOING SOLO

Other Running Press books by Ted Menten:

· · · · · · · · · · ·

*Gentle Closings: How to Say Goodbye
to Someone You Love*

*After Goodbye: How to Begin Again
After the Death of Someone You Love*

*Where is Heaven?: Children's Wisdom
on Facing Death*

GOING SOLO

....

Widows Tell Their Stories of Love,
Loss, and Rediscovery

by Ted Menten

RUNNING PRESS
PHILADELPHIA · LONDON

Copyright © 1995 by Ted Menten.
Printed in the United States. All rights reserved under the Pan-American
and International Copyright Conventions.

*This book may not be reproduced in whole or in part, in any
form or by any means, electronic or mechanical, including
photocopying, recording, or by any information storage and
retrieval system now known or hereafter invented, without
written permission from the publisher.*

Canadian representatives: General Publishing Co., Ltd.,
30 Lesmill Road, Don Mills, Ontario M3B 2T6.

9 8 7 6 5 4 3 2 1
Digit on the right indicates the number of this printing.

Library of Congress Cataloging-in-Publication Number 94–73892

ISBN 1–56138–655–0

Cover design by Toby Schmidt
Interior illustrations by Rosemary Tottoroto
Interior design by Susan E. Van Horn
Edited by David Borgenicht
Cover photograph copyright © Diane Petku/H. Armstrong Roberts

This book may be ordered by mail from the publisher.
Please add $2.50 for postage and handling.
But try your bookstore first!

Running Press Book Publishers
125 South Twenty-second Street
Philadelphia, Pennsylvania 19103–4399

This book is dedicated

with unending love

to the memory of

my aunt,

Gwendolyn Wadkinson,

who was

the merriest widow

of them all.

CONTENTS

PART

❶

What Is a Widow?

PART

❷

Ten Women

PART
3

Questions and Answers Over Coffee and Cake

Foreword

Undoubtedly, this book has found its way into the Self-Help section of your local library or book store. The term "Self-help" (which is usually short for, "Other People's Books That Tell You How to Help Yourself") is something of a misnomer—the word "help" itself implies outside intervention and assistance. A drowning person doesn't yell for self-help!

So even though the terms "Self-help" and "How to" have been applied to my books, I personally prefer the term "How You Might." I don't think anyone, especially me, is wise enough to know exactly how to solve anyone else's problems, but I certainly know how you *might* solve them.

If you're reading this book, you're probably looking for some answers to the problems a woman faces when she becomes a widow. But everyone is as unique as a snowflake, and no two snowflakes fall from heaven in exactly the same form. So despite that dress you saw last week that sported the claim, "One Size Fits All," there are no solutions that fit every problem. No easy answers to every tough question.

But I absolutely believe that experience is the best teacher, and this little book is filled with experience.

First and foremost, it's filled with the actual experiences of real women who became widows and had to deal with life after the man they loved died. And second, it's filled with my experiences listening to them and really hearing what they had to say. Whatever I know about them, they taught me.

I used to be an art director in a big company. On the wall behind my desk hung two signs. One read, IF YOU ARE NOT PART OF THE SOLUTION YOU ARE PART OF THE PROBLEM. The other sign read, DON'T TELL ME IT CAN'T BE DONE. JUST ADMIT *YOU* CAN'T DO IT. Those two slogans shortened my work load considerably.

If you feel that you need help, yell it out loud and clear. God and everyone else who loves you will be happy to assist. Even total strangers. (But beware of people and things that aren't part of the solution, like drugs and alcohol.)

And if you find yourself feeling that you can't do it, that it just *can't be done*, remember the little sign behind my desk and just admit you don't feel like *you* can do it—alone. Shout for help, seek it out, find it, and accept it. No one is so alone as the person who *thinks* they are.

Help is on the way. Maybe even in this little book.

Acknowledgments

My life, happily, has been populated with extraordinary women who not only loved me but taught me how to live and laugh. Many of them were widows, and they afforded me my first glimpse into the world of "solitaires":

My mother, Theresa, and her sister, Gwendolyn, as well as my two grandmothers, Laura and Anna, filled my early days with chocolate chip cookies and women's laughter.

Our neighbor, Lenore Woodard, an art teacher, discovered my early potential as an artist and nurtured it. My high school art teacher, Laura Strader, continued that work and added a sense of spirituality with her daily blackboard meditations. Florence Mills, the town librarian, continues to this day to keep me on my toes intellectually, and with her devotion and friendship, enriches my heart and mind.

My continuing friendship with my first working partner, Joan Shiel, is a daily reminder that men and women *can* be friends.

Cissy Dickson discovered me in the pages of *Gentle Closings*, sought me out, became my mentor, and foolishly allowed me to adopt her as the sister I never had.

And finally, Mary White-Williams gently led me into the world of the dying and showed me why I was sent here in the first place.

I thank them all, from the bottom of my heart.

Introduction

They come from everywhere—cities, towns, and tiny villages. They are young and old, rich and poor, some college educated and some high school dropouts. They are every color of the genetic rainbow. They are each unique, but they all have one thing in common—they are widows.

Webster's New World Dictionary defines a widow as, "a woman who has outlived the man to whom she was married at the time of his death." I'm sure most widows would have a great deal more to add to that definition. I define a widow more broadly: anyone who has lost a life partner, married or unmarried, female or male, straight or gay.

While the information in this book can be helpful to anyone who has lost a partner to death, I have chosen to focus only on married women, who have a more common and specific bond when grouped together and called "widows."

In 1991, after more than a dozen years of working with people facing death, I wrote my first book, *Gentle Closings: How to Say Goodbye to Someone You Love*. It was a book about love and heroism. It told the stories of both children and adults facing their approaching death and celebrating the life they had. And it was about those that they loved, and those who loved them, and how they all found a way to say goodbye.

And it was a book about teddy bears.

Like most people, I dislike hospitals. The few times I've had to visit them were painful, either physically or emotionally. So when my friends suggested that I join them for a visit to a hospital to give teddy bears to sick children, I naturally tried to find an excuse not to go. (Sooner or later you'll find out that I'm an old softie, so I'll fess up now and get it over with. I cry during *Lassie*, and during those telephone commercials in which the boy finally calls his mother on her birthday.) I'm the kind of guy Hallmark writes cards for, so the prospect of visiting sick children in a hospital was not high on my agenda. But, in the end, my friends convinced me, and my life changed forever.

I'm not a doctor, or a therapist, or a social worker. Everything I know was taught to me by experts—real people who were living the dying experience. They showed me what they needed and wanted as they faced the truth about life and death—their life, and their death. They taught me the importance of telling the truth no matter what the circumstances or aftermath. They taught me how to listen and actually *hear* them. How to hear what no one else wanted to hear, which was that they were dying. They were all great teachers, and from seven to seventy, their message was the same: "Life is wonderful!"

At first, I was helping people find a way to say goodbye to their loved ones. But the natural result of farewells is that someone is left behind. Many times, that someone became a widow.

So in 1994, I wrote *After Goodbye: How to Begin Again After the Death of Someone You Love*. In that book, the grieving tell their stories of sorrow and loss, and how, in time, they found their way back to new lives without their loved one. Once again, I was the student and the grieving were my instructors.

And now, on a gray winter's day, I am once again gathering together a group of teachers who are experts in their field.

We are sitting in a circle as we always are, and we sip our steaming cups of tea or coffee. After a few moments we settle down and someone gets us started.

Prologue: "Who Am I?"

"I used to love the holidays," says Jesse with a weary sigh. "But with Brian gone and Bobby off to college, it just seems like a cruel joke. We're still getting cards addressed to Mr. and Mrs. Johnson."

"Well, at least they aren't addressed to The Widow Johnson," quips Sophie.

"That's not funny. Most of the time I don't know who I am any more. At 42, I'm hardly a Miss, and this Ms. business is just too silly for me." Jesse takes a breath and continues. "I really hate the idea of saying that I'm having an identity crisis, but that's exactly what it feels like. I just don't know who I am any more. Am I still Mrs. Brian Johnson? Or am I just Jesse Johnson?"

"Who do you feel like?" I ask.

"No one," she replies, looking away towards the window.

"I know that feeling," offers Helen. "After ten years I'm still a widow and that's who and what I am. I used to be a lot of other things—but now I'm just a widow."

"I don't want that," says Jesse. "I just want to find out who I am, because until I settle that, I can't decide who I want to become."

"Honey, death took your man, and what you are is what you are. You didn't get to choose then and you don't now. What is—*is*."

"No, it isn't, Helen, not for me," replies Jesse. "I'm not going to spend years in limbo wondering what I'm supposed to do next."

"What do you mean by 'supposed to do'?" I ask.

"Oh, nothing as simple as, 'How long do I wear black?' Or, 'How soon is too soon to start flirting with men again?' Or when and if I should stop off at the beauty salon for a new hair color and style. I mean I need to find *me* in all this."

"You a grieving woman. A widow woman, like they usedta say," says Helen.

"Oh, Helen, that's not what I'm talking about. Widow is just a general term, like food. I need to be more specific. Am I meat or potatoes?"

"Keep going, Jesse," I urge.

"I'm not sure I know where I'm going with this. I only know that I need to know who I am now and who I will be in the future. Just saying I'm a widow isn't enough. Just saying that I *was* a wife isn't enough because a wife is as general a term as 'widow' or 'food.'"

"Yes, I know what you're saying now," offers Patricia. "A wife is many different things: partner, lover, confidante, playmate—the list is almost endless. When your husband dies, it feels like all of those parts of you have died too, and what is left seems like an empty shell. Kind of like a husk."

"Yes," replies Jesse. "And that makes me angry because all of those things were expressions of my love for Brian and expressions of me—as a person. With him gone now I feel that a large part of my emotional and intellectual vocabulary has been silenced. I look in the mirror and see only a partial person with no real identity."

"Are you suggesting that without a husband you have no identity?" I ask.

"No, no, no!" replies Jesse. "I mean that I have no one to express all that to. It's like talking to the wall. There's no response."

"There's an echo," I remark cryptically.

"What does that mean?"

"Well, if you say 'I love you' to the wall you'll get the same message back. It seems to me that you need to tell yourself that you love you."

"That's nonsense."

16

"No, Jesse, it isn't. When we love another person we have a whole list of reasons why. Sometimes we need to make that kind of list about ourselves as well. When we describe someone as *lovable* that means literally that they are *able to be loved*. That vocabulary that you say is missing is still there waiting to be used. Maybe right now you need an echo to remind you that *you love you*. We all know about all the side effects that the death of a partner brings with it. Anger, denial, self-pity, guilt, and a host of other feelings. Loss of identity is just another one of those side effects."

"But that still doesn't help me feel differently," cries Jesse. "I still don't know who I am."

"OK, Jesse, let's get very simple about this. If you left home this morning wearing a red scarf you might be described by all who passed you by as, 'A woman wearing a red scarf.' Now imagine that the scarf blows away. Now, the people who saw you wearing the red scarf might now describe you as, 'A woman who lost her scarf.' However, someone seeing you for the first time might describe you as, 'A woman in a gray coat.' But in all cases you are still a woman. You are always Jesse."

"So I'm a scarf widow, huh?"

"No, you're a woman whose husband died—and who still has her sense of humor."

WHAT IS A WIDOW?

Mister Bear and
the Journey to Harmony

As I mentioned earlier, I'm not a trained professional of any sort with fancy initials after my name. Of course, the kids have dubbed me *Mister Silly*, and a few of the doctors and nurses have a name or two for me that won't appear on my resume or in this book.

Among the older patients at the hospital, I am variously known as *The Teddy Bear Man, Mister Bear,* or just plain *Bear.*

I've written more than a dozen books about teddy bears, and the way I earn a living is by making them, one at a time, by hand. Believe it or not there is a whole industry out there that is entirely devoted to making and selling artist-created teddy bears—for adults.

All the work I do in Harmony is free. The teddy bears pay the rent.

When my first group of widows gathered together, I wondered how I'd feel about being there and I wondered how they'd feel about it as well. I was fairly comfortable about my role as facilitator and guide, but I wasn't too sure of myself as a counselor. I had certainly mastered the art of listening after working with the kids—but these were not children.

Or maybe they were.

For just as the children wanted a teddy bear to comfort them, the widows wanted something warm and fuzzy to comfort them. And so, I became Mister Bear. A kind of human Poppa Bear who had mastered the art of hugging and was always willing to listen. Mostly, I sit in my armchair, drink coffee, and nod with approval as they do all the work.

. . . .

When I started working with terminally-ill children, I felt that we needed a safe haven where we could always tell the truth—and face up to it when necessary. Out of that special need for safety and truth a mental space called Harmony was born.

We sit in a circle, hold hands, and breathe deeply until we all feel peaceful and connected. I called it breathing our way to Harmony, and it worked like magic, because it was. To me, anything that actually works is magical.

There aren't many rules in Harmony. We must always tell the truth—or what we think is the truth at the moment. We must always listen and not interrupt. And we never laugh or make fun of things we don't understand or agree with, because there may be great wisdom in what we are being told.

Harmony is wherever we sit together in a circle and listen to one another. And so, in my role as Mister Bear, I found myself sitting in a circle of women talking about finding their way without a partner.

In Harmony we search for the truth in many different ways. From time to time I become a surrogate for their husbands. We do confrontational work in which a widow gives me hell for dying, and I try to explain that it wasn't my fault that I died. But all in all, my role is a minor one, and today the groups work mostly on their own with very little help from me.

I feel a bit like Johnny Appleseed who planted the seeds. It is the trees that bear the fruit.

....

What Is A Widow?

A woman marries a man and becomes his wife. Throughout history that coupling has had a number of different meanings, but in modern times we consider a wife to be a partner. A wife may also be a mother, which is the female side of the partnership we call parenting. Some married couples are even in business together. In every case, she is a full partner. One half of a couple. Wife and husband.

But statistics inform us that most women outlive their partners.

When a husband dies, the partnership ends—and there is no longer a couple. And the survivor is called a widow.

I consider anyone—man or woman, straight or gay—who has lost a life partner to be a widow. But in most cases, a widow is a woman without a partner and is technically single—although hardly in the same way as an unmarried or divorced woman is. Mainly because it is not by choice that she is alone.

But she is alone. A widow is a woman alone—going solo.

When a pilot has completed flight training, the final achievement is to fly "solo." It is the final test and is the high point of training. It's a little like when the mother robin nudges her babies out of the nest and urges them to spread their wings and fly.

When a pilot or a baby robin flies on her own, she no doubt experiences a rush of excitement in that burst of freedom. And somewhere down below, someone is cheering that accomplishment.

To suggest that there is any similarity here to a widow may seem heartless, even cruel. This is not a moment of triumphant free flight to be cheered, but a heartbreaking, sad occurrence. Yes, the loss of a husband is very tragic, but it is not the end of the story.

It is the end of a chapter in that story. First came a chapter called Childhood, and another called Adolescence, and another called The Single Life and Dating. Then came a chapter called Falling in Love, and then Marriage, and then Parenthood.

In the perfect book of life there would be a chapter called

Growing Old Together. Then, many chapters later, there would be a brief chapter called Widowhood with only a few pages until the final words . . . The End.

But few of us get to live a perfect life's story, and when the chapter called Widowhood comes unexpectedly, the book needs a new conclusion.

This book is about writing those chapters of life that have yet to be written.

· ·

The Widow's Chain

Lots of wonderful books have been written about the process of grieving. In one way or another, they each speak about the process of reentry. Obviously, anything that deals with a process goes in *stages* or *steps*. Many self-help programs use a version of the twelve-step process that has been successful with people battling substance abuse.

Well, the Widows of Harmony have their own version of a step-by-step process. We call it The Widow's Chain.

A typical session begins casually. We gather, pour coffee or tea, snack a bit and then settle down in a circle. Some choose chairs, while others prefer a pillow on the floor. Then we talk, and talk, and talk, for about three hours. During that time we sense our growth—our forward movement in dealing with whatever it is we are dealing with.

At the end of the evening, we stand in a circle holding hands. At this point we speak our "word of remembrance." This is a single word or phrase that is all our own, and that we use to unlock all the memories of our loved one who is no longer with us in this life, but who remains within our heart and memory. It is a little formal ceremony of honoring and remembering, and is usually accompanied by free-flowing tears. Then we do some hugging.

Finally, we come to the chain. At this point the "senior" member of the group (usually the one who feels she is the furthest along) takes a step forward, reaches back, and pulls another woman forward—not necessarily the woman standing behind her. Then that woman reaches back and pulls another forward, and so on, and so on.

What is important here is *who* each woman chooses to pull forward. She chooses a woman she feels has made progress that day in her personal quest.

The gesture is one of recognition and affirmation. Sometimes, a woman resists being pulled forward and declines, insisting that she has made no progress. In Harmony, we accept this.

When the chain is completed we have a living, breathing testimony of our progress. But we do it one link at a time.

Searching For Solitaire

Louise Nevelson, the great American sculptor, once described herself as a *solitaire*—a beautiful, single gem in a golden setting. She was exactly that, and her monumental work demanded attention as powerfully as her own presence did.

If I have a single goal for the widows who come to Harmony it is that, in their own lives, they too will achieve solitaire status.

As I listen to the widows speak about their married lives and their grief, I see them as heroes. Not only have they survived the fire storm of death, but they have plunged back into the flames to save all that is precious to them.

I don't really like the term *survivor* applied to a widow because it suggests that they're victims and doesn't tell the true story. Yes, a widow has survived the death of her husband and, in that, she is a victim of circumstances. But she does more than merely survive. She goes on living, and that takes courage. That's the stuff of heroes!

After the death of her husband, a woman's life will never be the same. Everything will change, including her. So she can become a victim of her circumstances or she can become a champion overcoming seemingly insurmountable challenges. She can' wrap herself up in the widow's weeds of sorrow and self-pity, or she can remember and honor the love of her husband by living her life the best she can.

Finding solitaire may be the best thing a woman can do for herself, because it is about being just that—herself. It's about rediscovering herself and exploring her potential to its fullest.

As we will see, the choice is hers.

TEN WOMEN

Ten Women

Picture a comfortable, sunlight-filled room that has a clear view of green fields and rolling hills. There are comfortable chairs and giant pillows on the floor. Pots of flowers rest on top of polished tables. A huge fireplace dominates the far wall. On the sideboard, pots of tea and coffee brew, and the smell of freshly baked bread and blackberry jam fill the air. I have invited ten women to join me this afternoon. They know one another from Harmony and are anxious to share their experiences. The bell rings and I go to open the door.

Helen greets me with a bright smile and a hardy hug. Her husband died ten years ago and she is still dressed in black. Her skin is the color of milk chocolate and her dark eyes shift from bright and twinkling to dark and gloomy.

Huffing and puffing a few steps behind her is Sophie who, at 84, is husband-hunting at the banquet of life.

Margaret, her red hair tossed behind her, enters in a flurry. She is in her mid-thirties but carries herself like an old woman.

Next is Rachel, with her dark eyes and even darker disposition. She hugs me like a stranger and chooses a chair in the furthest corner.

Marie, her blond curls tied back with a ribbon, looks several years younger than she is. She and her husband grew up together in a small Ohio town and married after high school. He was killed two weeks after shipping out to Vietnam.

Patricia, dressed smartly in a gray wool suit, drops her briefcase by the door and hugs me warmly. I even get a friendly kiss on the cheek. "Sold the big one today," she whispers in my ear.

Terry, looking as lovely as ever, is close on Patricia's heels. They are both successful businesswomen who often go head-to-head on issues but can see themselves reflected in each other's lives.

Lisa slams the door of her old Ford twice before it closes, and hurries up the path. Breathless, she brushes back her gray-streaked brown hair and gives me a quick hug before heading straight for the coffee pot.

Laura, dressed casually in sweater and slacks, her straight blond hair cut short in a Dutch-boy style, kisses my cheek and hands me a bunch of daisies. "Nature's own. Stole them from a field down the road." She winks and joins the others.

Ten minutes later, Joan arrives.

"I'd about given up on you," I say.

"Oh, Poppa Bear, you know me. I never know until the very last second if I want to do this or not."

"Amen," chime in a few of the others.

Margaret

Margaret's disposition is as cloudy as an autumn day. Dark, brooding, and often sullen, she can't let go, can't accept that her husband is dead. It would be easy to describe her as a woman in denial, but that is too simple an explanation. Margaret is in a living nightmare, haunted by a ghost she believes is still alive.

"I saw Jack yesterday on the street," she says, recounting another sighting of her husband who has been dead more than two years. "He looked tired but handsome, as usual. He was wearing a green wool sweater. I never much cared for him in green, but maybe I'm wrong. I lost sight of him before I could decide. I thought about it all day and I still couldn't decide. Isn't that funny?"

"Did you ask him about the sweater?" inquires Patricia, who has the most understanding for Margaret.

"No, we didn't have a chance to speak."

"How are you sleeping these nights?" I ask.

"Well," she replies with a slight smile. "If you mean has Jack been naughty and dropping by, yes, he has."

"And?"

"We make love," she replies shyly.

"Margaret . . ." Patricia hesitates. "Jack is dead."

"I know that," replies Margaret in a tiny voice. "But *he* doesn't know it. He won't leave me alone. He's everywhere I go and at night he slips into bed beside me and holds me and makes love to me. I feel him. I smell him. His voice is in my head talking to me."

"What is he saying?" I ask.

"That he misses me. It's awful. He holds me and whispers that he misses me and then he asks if I miss him. How can he ask me that! I miss him constantly. I still set his place at the table. I never cook anything but his favorite foods. And he asks me if I miss him."

Tears stream down her face and her fists are tightly clenched.

"If I was the one who died I'd never ask him that. If I left him alone I'd never, never ask if he missed me. That's too cruel."

She doesn't bother to wipe away her tears. Patricia touches her arm, attempting to pull her out of this moment.

"Maggie, tell Jack to stop it."

"I can't," she sobs.

"Why not?"

"I want it too much." She buries her face in her hands and lets her tears flow uncontrolled. Patricia puts her arms around her and rocks her like a baby.

For a moment the room is quiet except for the sound of Maggie's tears. In one way or another, each woman in the room has had this experience. Not all are, or were, as tormented by these *sightings* as Margaret is. In time, the sightings are even welcomed as little reminders. We all enjoy things that remind us of pleasant things. The perfume that *she* wore, or *his* aftershave. A blond girl with a blue ribbon in her hair dashes up the steps of a museum and there *she* is again. A man bends down to light his pipe just the way *he* did.

At first, these moments are painful reminders of our loss. In time, they become blessings of remembrance. They are really wonderful when they come unexpectedly, like a surprise party. All of us know exactly how to trigger them. We touch an object, eat a special food, or drink that cocktail we had together the night we fell in love. We revisit special places. We sit by the grave and talk about what's happening in the world of the living. Remembering is honoring.

Margaret dries her tears and smiles at the group. She hugs Patricia and looks over at me.

"Tell me, old wise Mister Bear, will I ever stop this from happening?"

"Why would you want to?" I ask.

"What? This is crazy, isn't it?"

"Ladies?" I ask the group.

"No, child, it is not crazy," answers Helen. "Jack jes needs you to know he miss you. He keep fussin' with your head so you know he sorry for goin' off and dyin'. Gotta forgive him for that and then he be content. Gotta let that man go. You clutchin' too hard, honey."

"I used to yell at my husband every day after he died," injects

Sophie. "I yelled at him in life and I yelled at him in death. 'You putz!' I'd yell at him. 'Why'd you have to go off and leave me alone?' But I never meant it. I wanted him back every day, and I used every trick I knew to get him there so I could yell at him for leaving me."

"You jes needs some time, honey. Lord, it seem to take me forever to get that man to stop tormentin' me with my memories. Look at me, still in black. Still sitting in that same room he died in. Still grieving for a man ten years gone. Takes time, honey, lots and lots of time. I usedta feel guilty about taking all this time to grieve until Mista Smartypants over there told me to jes enjoy myself and grieve to my heart's content. Ain't content yet, but I working on it, honey."

"Some nights," says Margaret, pausing, "some nights I take a long bath and put on perfume and a pretty nightie and just wait for him. In the morning I feel stupid."

"Margaret," I say firmly. "Never feel stupid about loving someone. You and Jack were deeply in love and you miss him. That's about as natural as spring rain."

"But I keep imagining that I see him, that he's there with me."

"You just explained the whole thing yourself. You used the word *imagining* to describe what's happening. You *are* seeing Jack, not in reality but in your mind's eye. His touch that seems so real is your mind reminding your skin what he felt like, reminding your nose what he smelled like, your lips what he tasted like."

"But it is all so real—and so painful because it isn't real."

"Honey, what the hell is real anyways?" offers Helen. "I sure don't know. Stuff look real an' you reach out ta touch it and 'Poof!' It gone. Other stuff look fake an' 'Bam!' It hits you square in the behind. Maggie, honey, that boy loved you, an' that was so real it stayin' on after he gone. Cherish it. Wrap yourself in it, cause believe you me, if it go away—you in a lot more trouble than you are now."

Death

When people talk about death, there is always a great deal of conversation about God, faith, and prayer. My own experiences have led me to believe in all three.

I believe in a force beyond my comprehension that causes everything to happen, including things I don't understand. That list is a long one, and it includes sunsets, summer rain, pale pink roses, babies, electric light bulbs, and anything under the hood of a car. Only a supreme being could be responsible for those things, and while I might call that force God, you might call it Buddha or Allah, or something else.

I believe in faith, and faith comes to me in a number of ways. It is simply another word for everything that seems impossible, but is. Faith gets me from here to there. I love the expression "leap of faith," because it expresses the exact feeling I have every time I reject reason and go with faith instead. It is a giant leap—sometimes the leap of a dancer, sometimes the leap of a daredevil—but most often the leap of a fool.

I strongly believe in the healing power of prayer. I think it is much more sane to talk to someone else than to yourself. I pray all the time, in my mind—in a running dialogue with the part of my brain that argues with me about everything. And that's what God does, I think. God makes us reason with ourselves, reason with the little voice that tells us to rethink things. That's how God changes us.

And I believe that the only real death is being forgotten. Everyone I ever loved and who ever loved me is living safely in my heart and in my mind. And not just in my memory but in my living, active mind, my everyday working mind.

Peter Pan said that fairies died if you stopped believing in them. People die from being forgotten, too. The other side of that coin is that they can also live forever—in the hearts and minds of those who love them.

Think about this. A friend, living a great distance away, dies. You usually only call each other a few times a year, and so not hearing from your friend doesn't worry you. Then, months after the event, you hear that your friend died.

Here is the question: When did your friend die? On the date of the actual event or when you heard about it? Literally, on the date of the event—but emotionally, on the day you learned about it. Up until that moment, your friend was very much alive in your heart and mind. In fact, you had been collecting recipes to send her, and snapshots of your kids at Christmas. You had a bunch of stored memories that you wanted to share with her the next time she called. All of that time she was actually dead, but in your mind she was still alive. And, if you permit it, she will remain alive in your heart and mind until your day of reunion.

To some, death is the bogeyman. To others it is a blessing. In between those two extremes is every possible variation. We fear what we don't understand, and death is the great mystery. So is life.

We often forget that we die because we are supposed to—it is what living things do. Mostly, we get angry with death because it ends life, and we all love life. It's the party we never want to leave. When death threatens us or those we love, we become afraid and angry. No one wants to hear that the party's over.

I was twelve years old when my wonderful grandmother began her battle with cancer. Back then, there was little that could be done, so she was at home the whole time. She had a wonderful view of life that filled me with delight every day. She told me that death was the guy who tapped you on the shoulder and asked for the last dance. The final waltz of life. And she also commented that he was probably a pretty good dancer because he'd had a lot of experience. My grandmother was a wonderful dancer and I'm sure as they twirled away she whispered in his ear and made him laugh. At least that's the way I like to think it happened.

When the children get frightened of Mister Death, when they have bad dreams and bad days that might mean he is close by, I remind them of one of my mottos:

A dragon named is a dragon tamed.

Fear and death are nightmare creatures, dragons that need to be tamed and stilled. If you give a dragon a silly name like maybe "Wilbur" or "Willy," then how terrible can he be. I mean who could possibly be afraid of a dragon named Willy?

One of the kids asked me if I knew Mister Death's first name, and for a reason I cannot explain, I replied that I didn't know his first name, but I was positive that his middle name was "Oops."

When they all stopped laughing they asked me why that was his middle name, and I replied that Mister Death made mistakes just like everyone else. I think accidents are mistakes. I think near-death experiences are mistakes and that death returns people that he wasn't meant to dance with yet.

I think that death is that invisible little string tied around our finger at birth. It is placed there to remind us to live our lives wonderfully.

Helen

Helen reminds me of an overstuffed armchair or an old heavy cardigan sweater—she oozes comfort. Her bright smile lights up the room. Her black hair is faintly streaked with silver, and her bright brown eyes twinkle behind her wire-rimmed glasses. She is of my generation, in her sixties, and quick to remember the days before integration and the day they killed the dream, Martin Luther King, Jr. Born in the North, she still knew the stabbing pain of the word *nigger*. They didn't lynch black folks in her neighborhood, but they still hated them the same way. They even had their own version of the Klan.

She met Thomas when she was eighteen and he was twenty. They fell in love on sight and he made her giggle.

"Lord, oh, Lord, that boy could tickle me from a yard away. Jes make me go all silly inside like jelly in a bowl. Our folks thought we should wait, but we was hot an' in those days you didn't do it 'less you was married. At least, nice folks didn't, an' we was nice folks.

"We wanted children real bad but the good Lord didn't bless us, an' I'm too good a Christian to ask why—but I did wonder. Thomas always was a little boy in his heart and I expect that the Lord figured he was all the child I could handle in a single lifetime. That's what my Momma always said, but then she thought all men were foolish boys deep down. Can't say I disagree with her there.

"We were just decent, working-class black folks who loved each other and our families, and our church. Tommy and me jes went about our lives, livin' and lovin' and havin' a party every Saturday night. They usedta say that black people really *understood* Saturday night and I believe that's true.

"Then he started coughin' blood one night, an' the next thing I know he's laid out in a fine suit and some old lady is singing the blues. An' I realize that old lady is me.

"I've been wearin' black for ten years now, wrapped around my body and wrapped around my heart. Girlfriend of mine works at the hospital where old Mister Smartypants drops by now and again, an' she introduces us. Quick as a wink he's got me laughin' the way my Thomas did. Made me weep.

"So here I am tryin' to find my 'solitaire' in life. Tryin' to let go of Thomas. Thinkin' about buyin' a red dress."

She sits back and beams us a smile.

"Ladies," she continues. "Grief protects you against bein' alone. As long as I shed my tears for Thomas I couldn't be lookin' around for a new man to make me laugh. Woman from my generation all measured themselves by their men, an' a woman without a man had no measure. But a widow was protected by her grieving. Anytime someone say it time to go find another man I'd just start weepin' an' wailin' about Thomas and they'd leave me alone. Later on, I was just another widow woman that no one paid no never mind to. I was safe inside my black dress. The Mister calls it my suit of armor against the war of life. Mister Smartypants got sharp eyes."

Everyone laughs. Helen has her own set of names and endearments for me that the others enjoy but don't share.

"So," inquires Sophie. "You're maybe coming back to the banquet?"

"Could be, Sophie, could be."

"Listen, darling, I loved that sonofabitch with all my heart. Like the Bible says, right into my loins. I'm older than you—not too much—but older, maybe wiser too. I loved that bum from the moment I saw him, so good looking, so sure of himself. You think this one is a smartypants, you should have known my Avram. All the girls wanted him, but I got him. For years I was like you, dressed in black and fully protected against life. I was a weeping marathon. Finally, my granddaughter gave me a push out the door and here I am, back at the banquet. And you know what? I got boyfriends."

"Sophie," I interjected. "We all know you're a shuffleboard slut, but Helen isn't jumping on the next cruise ship for Bermuda."

"And why not? You think it all starts in the head, but I tell you if the body steps out the head will follow. You think that if I stopped to think about it I would have taken that first cruise? Not on your life. But my body went up the gangway and there I was.

And my head went along for the ride."

"Sophie, do they let black women on these cruises?" asks Helen.

"Of course, darling, why not? You could come as my maid."

They both scream with laughter and fall into each other's arms.

Grieving

Perhaps the most well-meaning but cruel remark one can make to a grieving person is, "Time to get on with your life."

A recent national survey revealed that most people feel that a month is a long time to grieve. I don't know who the survey takers interviewed, because I don't know anyone who stopped grieving after only a month. I would even go so far as to say that I don't know anyone who ever actually stopped grieving.

I wonder if you asked those same people how long you should rejoice after the birth of a healthy baby if their response would be a month. We rejoice over a healthy baby that grows up and becomes a healthy teenager, then a young adult, then a married person, then a parent, and then enjoys their golden years with a dozen grandchildren. We rejoice for that healthy baby every single day of their healthy life.

Until they die.

Then we grieve.

If we rejoice for life, why shouldn't we grieve for the loss of that life? And when the person who dies is a life partner, who is to say how long we should grieve *that* loss?

I want to stop a moment and discuss the word *loss*. When someone we love dies, we experience a loss. Not only the loss of that person but all that surrounded that person in life. We experience the loss of their love, and laughter, and intelligence, and support, and the thousand things they said and did that made them special. Loss is what happens to us and that loss is caused by death—nothing that we did.

So many times I hear people say, "I'm so sorry you *lost* your husband." Or even worse; "I'm so sorry you *lost* your child." First of all they are not lost, they are dead. And we who are grieving did not lose them—death *took* them!

I am not indulging in semantics or playing word games. We all know the subliminal message that words give. I have seen lives change in the turn of a phrase because that turn made a difference. It made someone see and hear that phrase in a completely new way, and that was the key that unlocked and opened the door to a new life.

I made this statement about the cruelty of that phrase ("I'm sorry you lost your child.") at a grief conference a couple of years ago. The room was filled with professional caregivers who had been working with grieving people for years. Afterwards, a middle-aged woman walked up and hugged me for setting her free. For years that phrase had haunted her—indicted her for what she knew was not her fault, though she somehow believed it was. Again and again she suffered the guilt imposed on her by that haunting phrase. By the evening's end, another dozen people repeated her experience almost word for word.

Grief, like joy, changes its shape from moment to moment. While we continue to rejoice in a baby's birth, we do it differently from day to day. The first few days after the event are a continuous party, but in time, that joy may simply be expressed by a sense of wonder and a constant smile on your face. And in time, even that will change.

Grief is not that different. The first few days after the event are filled with tears and sorrow, but in time the tears stop and the sharp pain becomes a dull ache. And in time, even that will change.

Life and death are both about time. Each person has a different timetable for life and for death. For rejoicing and for grieving.

The only rule is that there are no rules.

. . . .

Sophie

At 84, Sophie is a triumph over everything, at least according to her. According to Sophie, she is *very* Jewish—but since she isn't Orthodox I've never been sure what that means. Perhaps she means that she has more wisdom than a fortune cookie (which she claims she can outsmart with Jewish wisdom), or perhaps she is *very* Jewish because she can convince herself that her porkchop is really a lambchop. I can't begin to count the number of times the phrase ". . . for a very Jewish woman like me . . ." has cropped up in our conversations. Frankly, I have neither the energy or the space to transcribe that phrase as often as she uses it. So, for the full flavor of Sophie's story, the reader is encouraged to sprinkle that expression throughout her comments more than it already appears.

And so, without further ado, I give you Sophie: *a very Jewish woman.*

"You should have seen him, my Avram. Tall for a Jew and handsome like a store dummy. If I hadn't been such a good girl I would have wet my pants—he was that handsome. Every girl over the age of ten was in love with him. Come to think of it, the ones under ten loved him too.

"It wasn't easy, but I got him. My mother helped, of course. That's what mothers are for. She dressed me beautifully every day. She made friends with his silly mother and swore that if we got married she'd move away to avoid her. It wasn't true. They were crazy about each other and plotted every day to get us together. Every night she'd scream, 'How could such a crazy woman produce such a wonderful son?' I believed her, she was my mother. Down the street Avram's mother was screaming the same thing. He believed her, she was his mother. His mother praised all the other mothers of the girls that flirted with him but my mother was always 'that crazy woman down the street.'

We started meeting secretly and that probably drove them wild with happiness, but we never suspected.

"Not even when we got engaged did the charade end. Even the morning of the wedding my mother was calling her 'That crazy woman.' After the wedding I saw them hugging and kissing and giggling and I knew it was just like the tooth fairy—we'd been bamboozled.

"Avram was a perfect husband. Now I know you all say that your husbands were perfect and well, maybe they were, but for a very Jewish girl like me he *was* perfect.

"We had three sons and a daughter who died when she was six. Polio. We weren't the same after that, but we were still good together. After the kids grew up we used to carp at each other—but that was love too. Listen, he was still a hunk if you know what I mean.

"He dropped dead on the F train one morning. He was 62. I became the perfect widow. A very Jewish woman like me has to be— I was almost as good as my mother and she was perfect as a widow, like she was born for it. Darlings, she had it down pat, no rehearsing.

"Me, I modeled myself after her. My children were wonderful, and they offered to have me come live with them. What a nightmare. Grandma the baby sitter. No thanks, darling. I'll just sit here in my house and you visit. Visits I liked. Moving out, I didn't. Besides, in my house I could go on yelling at that bum for dropping dead on the F train and leaving me all alone. On the outside I was weeping, but on the inside I was mad as hell. We had a life together and it was a good life. So who needed to be a widow? I asked for this? I did not!

"The pain of it nearly broke my back. I ached from crying. I ached from longing. I wanted to be with my Avram. What was my life without him? Nothing, that's what! I'd yell for God to come and get me too, but the answer was always no.

"I'd get up in the morning and wander around the house touching everything he'd touched. Pain was my new companion and we went everywhere together.

"After ten years I was still in black—a little more fashionable, maybe, and some accessories too, but not much. Nothing gaudy, just gold. I played canasta with other widows. Big deal. I didn't have my Avram, but I had my pain.

"Then I took my first cruise. Darlings, that was my rebirth. New clothes, some new glasses, a rinse in my hair, red nails—and I was off to Bermuda. The first night, the Captain dances with me and I'm floating on air. Oh, the smell of that man drove me crazy. That night I told Avram that I still loved him but enough was enough and I was stepping out. And the rest, darlings, as they say, is history. Now I'm a naughty granny and a regular on the Love Boat.

"Every now and then I see some fella who looks like Avram and I get him out on the dance floor and curl into his arms and float away. I sniff his aftershave and let him twirl me around and around until I'm dizzy. Then I go back to my room and curl up in my bed and call to Avram, 'Hey, you dumb bunny, see what you're missing!' Then I snuggle my pillow and pretend he's there whispering in my ear and making love to me again just like he used to.

"Sometimes remembering is painful—but not as painful as forgetting."

Pain

Anyone who suggests that grieving is not genuine pain is a fool. Grief can bend you over and break your back. Grief is filled with aches and pains both emotional and physical.

If I'm working one-on-one with a grieving person I often suggest we take a walk together. This accomplishes two things. First, it gets the body into action. The lungs fill up and the blood flows. It clears the head of cobwebs, as my mother used to say. Second, it is a good, nonconfrontational way to have a conversation. Have you noticed how easy it is to talk to someone while driving in a car? Walking has the same effect. Things you might not say face-to-face over a cup of tea just flow out during a brisk walk in the park.

The word *healing* often crops up in discussions about grief. I'm not too comfortable with that concept. I don't like it when someone suggests that grief can or should be healed as though it were something to get over—like a cold.

Grief leaves scars, and some of them are big and ugly and very, very painful. Death is the cause, and we can't treat death because it's terminal. Death is a wound inflicted upon us. Grief is the healing process of that wound, and no matter how skillfully we treat that wound, there will be a scar.

Just as the initial wound of death is painful, the healing process is painful as well.

For example, you have an operation after a painful appendix attack. Even after the incision has been stitched, and even after the stitches are later removed and the incision is healed on the surface, there is still discomfort and pain.

When we suffer the wound of the death of a loved one, we enter into the grieving and healing process of life. It is neither easy nor painless, but it is necessary.

And people who delay their grief suffer more later when they confront their loss. Those who prolong their grieving in an unnatural way are picking at their scabs.

If we believe that grief speaks of our love for the person who has died, if we agree that they live on in our hearts, and if we understand that memory and remembering are ways of honoring the one we love, then maybe this is another way to think about the whole experience:

A few decades ago, young, European soldiers used to show off their dueling scars as a badge of honor. These scars, intentionally inflicted, and intentionally kept open until they finally healed in the desired disfigurement were but another example of scars interpreted as glamorization.

To grieve beyond the healing point is to pick at the wound and glamorize the scar.

Grief heals in its own time, in its own way.

· ·

Marie

Marie sits cross-legged on the floor, propped up on several pillows. Her blonde curls are caught behind her head and held in place by a robin's-egg-blue ribbon. It is *their* favorite color—Mark's favorite color.

She is the youngest in the group by a decade. Young enough to be the daughter or granddaughter of the others. I keep reminding them that she should not be pampered or fawned over, that in her grief she is their peer and equal. It doesn't always work.

Her green eyes turn gray when she is angry or sad. In the truest sense, they cloud over and reveal the darkness within.

Marie and Mark grew up together in a small town a few miles from Youngstown, Ohio. The families were good neighbors and good friends. They all went to church together on Sunday and shared

Thanksgiving and Christmas as a single family even before they were actually joined by their children's marriage.

If ever love was unquestioned it was between these two young kids. They married the day after high-school graduation. They planned to go to college together, but Vietnam interrupted their dream and Mark was killed shortly after he got to 'Nam.

Looking at her sitting on her pile of pillows, looking not much older than eighteen, I wonder if she bit her nails when Mark was alive.

Usually, these sessions flow on their own with one woman after another talking about what happened and where they are right now. But sometimes we hit a quiet spot where everyone seems to have gone inside for a moment and then I have to get things moving again.

"Marie," I ask gently. "Would you like to tell us about your trip last week?"

"Must I?" she inquires like a little girl not wanting to do her show-and-tell.

"I think so," I reply in my best fatherly tone, matching her game.

"I went to Washington," she remarks flatly. "To the Wall. To see Mark."

It is more than a decade since Mark died, but it might as well have been yesterday for Marie. Her youthful appearance is not the only thing about her that is unchanged. She is still living in the past, still married to Mark. Wife, not widow.

"Oh, honey," croons Helen, knowing I will disapprove of her big momma voice. She catches my eye and backs off.

"I went to Washington last year for the Quilt ceremony," remarks Joan, whose husband died of AIDS. "It's a pretty city."

Marie continues. "The whole family went. My parents, his parents, his sisters, and their [she pauses] husbands." She holds her knuckles against her mouth and continues. "I hated every moment of it. We stopped to buy flowers and I waited in the car. I'm such a bitch. No one said anything, you know, they never do. I'm excused because I'm a grieving widow.

"That's a joke. What I am is a raging, pissed-off bitch! And everyone knows it and pretends not to. Anyway, we got there and it wasn't what I expected at all. It's horrible. It's this long, black slab half buried in the ground. It's monolithic, like that slab in the movie *2001* pushed over on its side. I hated it on sight.

"Then began the search for his name. It reminded me of a scavenger hunt and I refused to join in their game. My mother stayed with me. I don't know what she thought I was going to do. Maybe she thought I'd finally cry. She'd like that, but it wasn't very likely to happen. I have never cried for Mark. I'm too pissed-off at him for being so stupid, so patriotic. We were married and going to college. He could have been deferred, and if he wasn't deferred we could have gone to Canada. But not him, oh, no. Mister all-American boy had to go and get his brains splattered all over some damn rice paddy.

What a jerk. I married an idiot. Look at me, I'm the idiot's widow. Want a laugh, ladies? I was a virgin when we got married. I can count the times we made love on one hand before he was in his macho Marine uniform straining at the bit to ship out. The man was a total jerk. He was only a *boy*—he hardly ever shaved."

She jumps up and paces in a circle and then sits back down.

"Sorry," she continues. "I'm supposed to be talking about our family outing in Washington, D.C., the capitol of our great nation. Actually, it's kind of fitting. It reminds me of what my sweet Christian mother used to do when the neighbor's dog 'made a poop' on our front lawn. She'd pick it up in a white paper napkin and put it on their front stoop."

We all laugh along with her.

"So there we are, the families of the dead hero, looking for his name on this ugly monolith—this napkin-wrapped poop on the front yard of our great nation's seat of government. Seems fitting to me.

"Well, after what seemed like eternity, they found his name and everyone, except me, gathered to lay their flowers. My mother asked if I wasn't going over too, and I said no. She left me standing there and went to do her thing.

"I looked around and there seemed to be dozens and dozens of people doing the exact same thing, looking for a loved one's name and then touching it when they discovered it among all the thousands of others. There were guys my age, scruffy types with long hair and beards, a few on crutches or in wheelchairs, looking for their buddies. I wondered about them. I wanted to get inside their heads and figure out their macho stupidity."

I watch her hands as they clench and unclench in a repeated gesture of rage. She starts rocking back and forth as the memory grows more vivid.

"Finally, mercifully, we left, went back to the hotel, and went to bed. I'm a light sleeper, and the sounds of the city kept waking me up. Toward dawn, I got up and dressed, and went downstairs in search of coffee—but instead I found myself calling for a taxi to take me back to the memorial.

"In the gray, early morning light I searched for his name—and finally found it just as the sun broke over the trees. I just stood there like a statue. I wanted to feel something, anything. Sorrow. Pain. Anger. Anything. But nothing happened. I told myself I was a cold and heartless bitch, filled with rage and self-pity. I stood there hating a boy I had loved all my life. A boy who loved me, me, the bitch.

"Without knowing why, maybe because I'd seen others doing it, I reached out and touched his name, ran my fingertips over the engraving, until suddenly I was deafened by my own screaming. I was on my knees in all the family flowers, pounding my fists against that horrible stone slab. Beating my fists on his name and screaming at the top of my lungs that I hated him for leaving me, for getting himself killed in that meaningless rice field. And I was crying. Tears streamed down my face, snot came out of my nose, I drooled through my screams until my throat was raw. I cursed in words I didn't realize I even knew. And I kept on pounding that wall with my fists until I was exhausted and crumpled over on my hands and knees.

"I don't know how long I was there, but I felt someone touch my shoulders and lift me up and embrace me. It was my mother. She followed me there. She held me in her arms and said those mommy words, 'There, there, it's going to be all right.' She stroked my head, held my shoulder and guided me down the pathway, away from the wall."

We all sit silently while Marie rocks back and forth in her memory. Tears streak her cheeks once again and after a few moments she smiles at us.

"Thank you all for being here and listening."

Tears

I love tears. To me, they are like a gentle rain that refreshes the air and blesses the earth. And I love both tears of joy and tears of sorrow because they tell me I'm alive and have feelings. Not being able to shed tears can be a terrible burden.

Traditionally, especially in America, men are taught not to cry, not to be "cry babies." But holding back tears is not the exclusive domain of the American macho man. Many women cannot—or will not—shed their tears. For reasons I can neither understand nor explain, we uphold the code of the "stiff upper lip." We watch beautiful Jacqueline Kennedy, swathed in a black veil with no visible emotion on her face and we call her "noble," and "brave," and "heroic."

That may be the desired demeanor for a First Lady, but I personally prefer a lot of weeping and wailing and rending of garments in the Old Testament tradition. I follow Shakespeare's advice from *Julius Caesar*, ", , , if you have tears to shed, prepare to shed them now." And I encourage both men and women to shed their tears.

Tears are a release that relieves the stress of grief. I have often wondered if people hold back their tears to avoid the release. Are they, I wonder, holding on to the pain? Many times the answer is yes, and perhaps the most common reason for that is "survivor syndrome."

Millions of Jews perished in the death camps of Hitler's Germany. When the survivors were rescued, many had no tears for their friends and family who had perished. They felt guilty because they had survived. They were not entitled to tears. They were not entitled to *shed* their grief.

Survivors of plane crashes, earthquakes, drowning incidents, and a hundred other deadly experiences, can suffer the same fate. They feel they don't *deserve* to be alive. They don't *deserve* to be able to shed their tears.

And women who *survive* their husbands often share this feeling. Once again, we see the cruelty of commonly used expressions. Obituaries usually use expressions like, ". . . survived by his loving wife and four children." That phrase suggests that death visited them all, but only took the husband/father, and the rest of the family *survived* the disaster. They got lucky, as the saying goes.

But that isn't what happened at all. Death came for one person and only one person. No one got lucky or was *spared*. Still, the subliminal messages suggest otherwise, and very often a widow unconsciously reacts by feeling that she is a very different kind of survivor.

In my opinion, too many people talk about survivors in the world of grief. I have done it myself. The difference is whether you consider them to be victims or champions. Many survivors of the concentration camps emerged as lifelong victims, while others emerged as champions. The victims thought they had *escaped*, while the champions knew they had *triumphed*.

When death comes in the room, we all hold our breath. And when he chooses someone else for the last waltz, we breath a sigh of relief that he has not chosen us, even if he has chosen someone we love. Like it or not, we are human, and being human means we want life.

If we did not want it, we would not be alive in the truest sense.

Joan

If you saw Joan on the street you'd probably assume she came from a good middle-class family, had gone to college, married her high school sweetheart, and had two-point-five children, two dogs, and a cat. You would probably admire her fresh beauty, her clear blue eyes, and her perfectly tailored clothing. You might even be envious of her.

Joan *is* exactly what she appears to be, a nice, well-educated, working mother of two, with several pets, and a station wagon. She lives with her children in a quiet community where there is lots of lawn between the ranch-style homes.

And seeing all this, you might wonder why she and her children drove to Washington, D.C., to witness the laying of The AIDS Quilt.

"We worked on Kenny's panel for about a month," Joan began. "The deadline for getting it to The Names Project was still weeks away, but we wanted to be sure it was included. We wanted Kenny's panel to be there when we went to see the ceremony.

"The kids were great and did most of the fabric cutting while I pinned and pasted and finally sewed the letters that told his story. 'Beloved Husband and Devoted Father.' His name and dates were surrounded with drawings the kids had made, and snapshots from our family album were sewn down under plastic. A couple of gay guys from one of the local AIDS support groups came by to help us with the technical part, like the plastic covering. They had a lot of experience and were a great comfort. I wonder now how I could ever have hated them."

"Why would you hate them?" asked Sophie.

"I didn't know until he got sick that Kenny was bisexual."

"Well, that's a double whammy," said Patricia.

"More like a triple. I didn't know that, and I didn't know he had AIDS, and now I don't know if we do. When he first told me I was pretty calm about it, because he wasn't really sick yet and his relationships with men all happened before we got married. I understood Kenny and I could see how he might have been confused about his sexuality. During the 1970s there was all that sexual freedom and experimentation, and with women demanding their rights and almost refusing to be women in a traditional—even old-fashioned—way, I could understand how a boy like Kenny could be confused.

"But, in time, I also realized that he had actually wanted those relationships and that he had really cared about those men. That frightened and infuriated me because I couldn't understand *that*."

"Honey, love be blind," said Helen softly. "Praise the Lord for that. Love don' care about color, or age, or who is who, or what is what. God made us all different, but He gave us all the gift of love an'

He told us to share it. Honey, think about this: Kenny loved those boys. He wasn't jes messin' around. He had good feelings an' good intentions. You may not like that but if it be me, I'd be proud to have a man that did what he did, right or wrong, 'cause of love."

"Don't worry, Helen, I finally got to that place myself—but it took time and it wasn't easy. I had a lot of denial and anger about everything, especially his death. The children were still too young to understand what was happening, and that was a blessing. We had plenty of time to prepare them—or so we thought. And hoped.

"We all got tested for AIDS, and we were all negative—but that's no guarantee. We go back every year now. At first we went every three months. I wanted to go every day.

"We didn't tell anyone. We didn't even use our family doctor for the tests. We went to the city for all our medical needs. I wasn't naive enough to believe my friends and family or our community would understand. I had seen plenty of stories on TV about the treatment AIDS patients got from their friends and family and, worst of all, the medical community. One day we're a Norman Rockwell painting and the next we're in *The Twilight Zone*.

"We went through all the stages that Kubler-Ross describes in her books. I used to get enraged at people who said that death was a blessing. *Life* is a blessing. Death is a tragedy. But even that idea changed.

"I did some work with AIDS patients because I needed to understand and I needed to be prepared for the worst. It was horrible and I was terrified. Terrified for Kenny and for myself and for our children.

"I will never say that death is a blessing, but it is a mercy. Swiftness *is* a blessing, and Kenny was blessed with a quick death. He contracted pneumonia and died two weeks later. No one knew it was AIDS. I often wonder if they would have all been so loving and supportive if they had.

"I was still dragging around a lot of anger and fear. At night I'd lay in our bed and remember how wonderful he was, what a good friend, and tender lover. And suddenly I'd see him with men and I'd scream out loud at him. I saw a talk show about bisexual men and some stupid woman in the audience stood up and said, 'At least it wasn't another woman.' And I thought, you stupid bitch, I could compete with another woman but not a man. I wasn't even sure what they did together. And I didn't want to know.

"I began to feel like a criminal in the witness protection program, always afraid of discovery. I sold the house and moved to the city. The kids are in a good school, but they miss the yard. It all takes time.

"So we went to Washington to see the Quilt. It was the most profoundly moving experience I have ever had. Young men and women, dressed in white, unfurl the quilts and gently lower them to the ground. Each quilt is made up of a number of squares and there are pathways between quilts. In the background, people read aloud the names of friends and loved ones as hundreds of silent, grieving people slowly walk between the panels.

"So much pain and so much love gathered in one place. After an hour or so, we found Kenny, and we just stood there and cried. All around us people were doing the same thing. The children were wonderfully behaved. They seemed to understand everything that was happening.

"I was standing there with tears streaming down my face, and still I was filled with anger and fear. All I wanted to do was scream from pain. And in the midst of all this, a voice called my name and I turned to face a total stranger who was holding out his hand to me. He smiled and introduced himself. 'I was in the bed next to Kenny the first week he was in the hospital. I recognized you and the children the minute I saw you this morning, but I was working with the quilts and this is the first chance I had to come over. I guess I feel as though I know you and the kids because that's all he ever talked about. He was a great guy. I'll miss him.'

"He hugged me and he hugged the children and then he was gone. Like the other workers, he was dressed all in white, and as he walked away I felt as though I had been hugged by an angel.

"And then my little girl asked who the nice man was, and I answered that it was one of daddy's friends. And for the first time, I understood everything."

Fear

The legacy of death is loss, and the companion of loss is fear. Like a macabre version of Tweedle Dee and Tweedle Dum, these two fellows conspire to mess up our lives if we let them.

In the aftermath of her husband's death, a woman is faced with a host of decisions to make and problems to solve. Already overwhelmed, she is asked to do things she may have neither the strength nor the knowledge to do.

Usually, the first question is about money—is there enough? Enough to bury her husband? Enough to pay the bills? Enough to keep the home? Enough to eat? But even if there is more than enough to take care of all these needs, she will still fear that it won't be enough. That's human nature. It is human nature to feel that there isn't enough of anything when you have just suffered the loss of your husband, partner, and lover.

Loss opens the door, and fear walks right in. These uninvited guests are here to keep you company in the days after your husband dies. And what rotten guests they are—always nagging at your mind, telling you how alone you are, and how nothing will ever be the same again. They are there with you night and day, awake or asleep. And if you let them, they will take over and never leave.

But like all bad house guests, they serve a purpose. It is better, healthier, to feel your loss than it is to deny or suppress it. Despite all the new demands placed on you as head of the house, you must take time for yourself. Time to grieve, time to think without interruption or without outside counsel. No matter how many loving, well-intentioned people gather you in their arms and tell you they'll help, you will ultimately have to do it for yourself and by yourself. So, take the time to be alone and think about how you feel and what you want. It will not be easy, that much I can promise you. But it is the most important thing you can do for yourself.

You will find that many fears are best defeated by giving them an accurate name.

If your big worry is money, then rename it "budget," and break it down into smaller bits of worry with accurate names. Some aspects of money are assets and some are liabilities. Again, break these down. How much money is in the bank? Insurance. Stocks and bonds. Real estate. Valuables. How much money is in liabilities like house payments, hospitals, credit cards, and the kids' tuition?

Don't let fear become your bookkeeper or your financial advisor. Don't let loss blind you.

We know that fear gives us a rush of adrenaline that charges us up. Some studies even show that worry does a similar thing. People who were "so worried I couldn't sleep" often found that they weren't actually tired the next day. Their worry had charged them up in the same way sleep did.

So once you accept the fact that those two bums (loss and fear) are going to be around for a while, you can start to dust around them.

My grandmother, in a slightly more graphic form, used to say that dog doo-doo with a pink bow on it was still doo-doo. And, as usual, she was right. You can't hide the truth, and you can't dress it up, because sooner or later you'll discover it is what it is. And if it's doo-doo, it will probably stink.

....

Patricia

Patricia returns to her chair after a cigarette break outside. She smoothes her tailored skirt and stirs her coffee. At 42 she is in her prime, physically and in her career. Not exactly beautiful, she is what is often referred to as a *handsome* woman. While that seems to imply a slight masculine appearance, nothing could be further from the truth. Patricia is all woman—but she has that edge that lets you know she is strong. She is like a pioneer woman in a Bill Blass suit.

She and her husband ran a successful real estate business together, and after his death, despite everyone's advice to the contrary, she kept the business and runs it by herself. At first glance one might say that

Patricia is the perfect example of a young widow who pulled herself together and was going solo in style.

But that would only be at first glance.

"Well, Patricia," I ask. "How is Howard today?"

"Howard is losing his hair, has developed a gut, and is playing tennis in an attempt to stay young looking. I don't mind the receding hairline, but the gut has to go."

Her little game is about what Howard might be like today if he hadn't been careless and died. Patricia firmly believes that a lousy diet killed him.

"And you?" I inquire playfully.

"I have all my hair and no belly, at least no belly under my panty girdle."

"I see."

"I hope not! Anyway, it doesn't matter because I'm the only one who sees it these days."

"What happened to Jeff?" I ask referring to her boyfriend.

"Recent history. I thought he said he wanted *boobies* but what he really said was *booty*. A gold digger, girls. A bum."

"But a man," says Sophie.

"Oh, God, Sophie, take a cruise. I swear you are the horniest old broad I ever saw. Do you really want another man in your life?"

"No, darling girl, I want a dozen. So there. I *am* a horny old broad, but I'm not wasting away with my juices drying up."

"What! You're a terrible old bitch to boot. I am not drying up, you old tootsie. I am as juicy as ever."

"Sez who?"

"Says me."

"Let me hear it from a man."

"Sophie, men are not the whole thing in life. There are lots of other things."

"Mechanical devices don't count."

"Sophie," I interject. "Put a cork in it!"

"OK, OK but that girl is wasting time and she'll regret it. She looks good now, but pretty soon she'll start to melt and look like an old candle. Of course, that ain't so bad. Look at me, I still burn pretty bright. Anyway, she needs to think more about her life and less about her business."

"My business *is* my life right now."

"Too bad," persists Sophie. "A fella would be better."

"Listen to me, Ms. My-candle-burns-at-both-ends, I am doing just fine. I loved my husband and he loved me, and we built a business together and I happen to think that by continuing on with that business I am honoring him. I kept our home and I kept our business because I love all the memories in those places. It doesn't make me sad to be there, it makes me feel good. I miss him terribly, but I talk to him every day. I share everything with him. I think about what he'd be like now. And it isn't morose or morbid."

"A ghost," snaps Sophie.

"No, Sophie, a healthy memory."

"One question, please."

"What?"

"You ever bring another man home with you?"

"No."

"I rest my case," Sophie folds her arms over her chest. She is finished for now.

"Let's move on now that Perry Mason is done," I suggest. "Patricia, do you feel that you are a happy, solo person, maybe even a solitaire?"

"I'm close, but I won't say I'm there yet, and Sophie is partly right—but not about the bedroom. I miss cooking for Howard.

"I miss picking up after him. I miss beating him at chess. I miss his laughter. And I miss his body, his physical presence. I miss him *being* there.

"After he died I had to totally start over socially. Our friends were just that, *our* friends. Not mine or his but ours, like everything else in our lives. After he died, half of what everyone loved about us was gone and I was just a reminder of what they'd lost too. Everyone was very kind and loving and supportive and all that, but it just wasn't the same. It just didn't work anymore.

"So I simply started over. I slowly replaced everyone at the office because I wanted a staff that worked for me, and not for me-and-the-remembrance-of-Howard. I got involved in new groups and activities and I even went on a few dates.

"Howard wasn't perfect. Hell, I'm not either. But *we* were. We were a good fit, and that isn't easy to find again. Most days I feel like half of a person—but then I talk to him and I get his opinion, I just tap into my memory banks and I *know* what he'd say.

"Am I going solo yet? Yes, I am. Am I a solitaire yet? Well, let's just say I'm a work in progress."

Loneliness

Obviously, after the death of someone we love, there is bound to be a period of loneliness. Usually, the form of loneliness changes as the various stages of grieving affect it. But there is a great difference between being alone, being lonely, and loneliness.

Garbo wanted to "be alone"—although many say that she actually said, "I want to be left alone," and considering her reclusive nature, that might be a more accurate quote. But either way, it was her choice to be alone.

Being alone as the result of your partner's death is quite another thing.

Being lonely suggests a certain wistfulness that implies a desire to be invited over for tea or out on a date.

Loneliness is a much darker, brooding thing that engulfs us like a dense fog and impairs our vision and movement.

When I first sat down with my editor to discuss this book, my first idea was to write a book for anyone who had suffered the death of a life partner. But as we talked, it became clear that married women had more and different problems than either live-in lovers, or a gay couple.

Most of those special problems center around the fact that they were married. A married *couple*. For reasons beyond my ability to explain, unmarried couples are considered two individuals in a pair. Married couples are considered a single unit, separated only by divorce or death.

The divorcee and the widow share a number of social stigma, including no longer being welcome at dinner parties for married couples.

Of course, no one really admits this and invitations to lunch by old married friends abound. But those dinner parties are a real problem.

"Should we invite Janet?" "Is she still mourning?" "Has she started dating again?" "Do we know any nice men?"

Lunch is easier.

Just when the widow needs company most it seems to evaporate like the morning dew.

Widows aren't like single women or even divorced women. Widows are not alone by choice, and that makes a hell of a difference. Being single and not having a date for New Year's Eve is hell. But being a widow alone on New Year's Eve is HELL in capital letters.

Every day, in a hundred subtle and a few not-so-subtle ways, a widow is made to feel like an outcast by those she thought were closest to her. Her loneliness and her sense of being excluded cause her grief to be that much more painful. A widow will tell you that the Christmas card list got a lot shorter a year after her husband's death.

She is in a no-win situation. She's wrong if she doesn't grieve long enough. She's wrong if she grieves too long. So since everyone has their own agenda for grief, the widow becomes a culprit who has committed no crime.

What I find interesting is that this attitude is not confined to young widows. One 70-year-old widow told me that her friends chastised her for not dating and getting married again. This nonsense started a month after her dear husband was buried. And she is no exception. Actually, women from generations prior to the 1960s were almost exclusively defined by their marital status. No wonder they wanted their friend to find a new man. How could she possibly exist without one?

Loneliness is like a knife in the heart, but more often than not, it feels like a knife in the back.

Lisa

Outside the shadows are lengthening and most of us are drinking our third cup of coffee. Lisa is working on her fifth. I guess Lisa is in her fifties. She's a bit overweight, has gray streaks in her hair, and more than a few frown lines. It might be easy to say that life has been hard on her but the truth is, she's hard on herself, and everyone else. She reminds me, at times, of my old math teacher who was prone to cracking knuckles with a steel-edged wooden ruler. To call her stern would be a compliment. But, unlike my math teacher, Lisa has a soft center.

"That old car is falling apart, just like I am," she says, brushing back a wisp of hair from her high forehead. "I go on, it goes on, but we both need a serious tune-up. And a new coat of paint." She smiles and shrugs. "I just wake up tired every damn day. I don't know how Helen and Sophie have so much energy for living. It knocks the wind right out of me.

"Peggy and the boys are all away at school now and I can actually put my feet up and take a breather. But give me five minutes alone and I'm having that same old conversation with Joe about the night he died.

I just wish I knew what really happened. I wish Peggy could remember and tell me. Sure, I know that's selfish. I should thank the Lord He took *that* memory from her. I praise Him for sparing her that pain, that awful memory of her dead daddy. But I still wish I knew. The not knowing is what's so awful. I mean, could it have somehow been prevented?

"That cow of a sister of mine keeps saying it was God's will and I tell her it will be more than God's will if she finds my fist in her mouth. Sweet Jesus, I love my family but they've got a stupid streak right through the middle of them. God gives us life and death takes it away, and that's that.

"My brother keeps bringing home husband material for my consideration and that's about as foolish as one boy can get. Who would marry me?"

"Darling, you could look terrific with a little attention to grooming," Sophie said.

"Dear, Sophie, you have a bobby pin for every woe. I do love you but shut up please. I am not marriage material. I wonder if I ever was. You know, I was pretty independent in my youth. In fact that's what got me married. I wanted to be independent of my family. There's a joke for you."

"Lisa," I interrupt. "What about the night Joe died?"

"Oh, God," she heaves a sigh and squares her shoulders as if she is getting ready to endure something, an interrogation maybe. "Peggy was sixteen and at a friend's house. She called me to come and get her but I was making dinner so I sent Joe. The next thing I know the police are standing on my porch telling me Joe is dead and Peggy is in a coma. I just followed them down the steps and into their car. Every pot on the stove burned while I was gone.

"Peggy stayed in the coma for six weeks and when she woke up she didn't remember anything. The nagging problem was who was actually driving. In other words, who killed my husband, my daughter or the jerk himself? The police also wanted to know, which I suppose was so that they could charge my daughter after she came out of the coma. Who knows? For some reason, Peggy was thrown clear but was on the driver's side of the car a few yards away. Joe was hanging out of the driver's side, but at an odd angle that suggested he had somehow slid across the seat from the passenger side. One cop suggested that Peggy was driving and lost control and that Joe tried to slide over and take control—but was too late. Everyone knew he was teaching her to drive. It was a real possibility that she was driving. And for a long time I blamed her. I never accused her to her face—but in my heart I blamed her. So did her brothers. We had a lot of ugly time together blaming each other. Maybe I should have gone and not sent him. He'd had a beer before dinner, maybe two. Who knows, besides God? And He hasn't told me, but I ask.

"When I wasn't angry with Peggy, or myself, or Joe, I grieved. I wept. I cursed. And I wept some more. I had a little falling out with God and I nearly punched a priest for being really stupid, a jerk.

But that all passed and I told God I was sorry but I refused to forgive that priest. What kind of jerk says, 'Be grateful to God that He didn't take your daughter too.' I should have blackened both his eyes for that remark. What a comfort he was.

"The rest of my family was asking me what I was going to do. I guess they were afraid we'd move in with them. Lovely bunch they are.

"I dried my tears and went to work. Two jobs. A Chinese laundry by day and a barmaid at night. It was different. The laundry was great—they hardly spoke English so I didn't have to talk to them. The bar was OK because no one came in to hear my sad story. They had their own. Some of them were doozies and made me feel like I got off lucky.

"My kids all did well in school, got scholarships to college, and are working to make up the difference. I'm still working too, but now I'm in computers. I went to night school and learned. It's the future, and that's what I need, a future.

"I guess I'm making progress. I feel like I am and I'm no longer at the end of the chain. Maybe when Helen gets her red dress or Sophie catches her man, I'll take over one of their links in the chain.

"I lost my husband—sorry—*I experienced the loss of my husband* and it nearly destroyed my family. I fell out with God but found my way back. I kept it all together—and one of these days I'm going to be a solitaire."

Family

When death takes any member of a family, the entire family is put in disarray. All the interactions change, all the balances of power and responsibilities shift from one member to another, depending on who has died.

While the death of a partner can be devastating to the remaining partner, that pain and loss can also be intensified by the loss the children feel when Mommy or Daddy dies.

When Daddy dies the household often loses much more than a father figure. Often that loss is accompanied by loss of income, perhaps even the family home. A woman with children is a widow with problems that reach way beyond grief.

In times of grief we hope to find support from those who love us, friends and family. But when that isn't possible, when there is no family, and friends are unable to do much more than occasionally baby-sit so that the widow can have a quiet moment to herself, the problem becomes intense.

The common fantasy is that a couple grows old together and when one dies the other is supported by their children. It happens, but other things happen too. Every day young men die and leave behind young wives and young mothers. With street violence and disease on the rise, these numbers are increasing.

I'm sure that the word "widow" does not evoke an image of a 23-year-old girl with two babies to care for, but there are many widows out there that fit that description. Every time we send young men overseas for a "police action," the population of young widows increases. Today, sadly, death comes too easily and too early.

Even more heartbreaking is the family tragedy in which several members are involved in the deadly event. Blame and guilt are heaped on top of grief in a backbreaking drama that can only produce more pain.

The headlines are filled with these events. The house that burns and kills a mother and two children. A boating accident in which one brother drowns and the other survives. A private plane crashes. Accidents in the schoolyard. The gun they thought wasn't loaded. Every day another story of a family torn apart by the event of death.

The family, the very symbol of all that should be safe and secure, is suddenly shattered. A house of cards that collapses when one card is suddenly pulled away—by death.

Laura

Laura's short blond hair and her clear blue eyes made me feel eighteen again. She smelled of springtime and always dressed like a young Kate Hepburn. She's like the girl in the J. Crew catalog who looks all fresh and scrubbed and ready to go sailing at the drop of an anchor.

Laura refers to herself as the twenty-minute widow. A description filled with bitterness.

"I was a widow longer than I was a bride," she says with a playful smile. She is sitting on the floor hugging her knees and being a little less than serious about her pain.

"The entire business took little more than a year. A few weeks of flirting. A few more shopping for a suitable outfit. A few weeks of honeymoon bliss. A few more of marriage and domesticity and then wham, bam, hello widowhood. Trust me, that's one year for the record books.

"I was a terrible widow. Actually, I was too stunned to really pull it together. At the wake I kept saying 'Thank you for coming' in a tone that sounded more like this was a graduation party instead of a send-off for my dear departed husband, what's-his-name. I was awful. I was head over heels in love with him, with his eyes, and hair, and body and I didn't know or care if he had a brain in his head. Of course, he was smart as a whip, but I'm telling you I didn't care because he could set me afire from across the room. If the man hadn't married me I'd have kidnaped him and kept him in slavery. Sounds good doesn't it, Sophie?"

Sophie nods approvingly and Laura continues.

"Well, when he died I was naturally shaken, but I also felt cheated by it. It's like buying your dream car—and it turns out to be a lemon. Oops, bad taste joke. Anyway, I cried and cried and cried some more and then I went and got a haircut and my nails done because that always makes me feel new again. I needed that, because right then I looked and felt pretty beaten up. I decided to get away and pull myself together, so I went to Paris where I met Charlie and married him a week later. Ladies, pleeeze don't rush to judgment. Actually, Charlie is a dream come true. The trouble is with Dave, my first husband. He won't move out of my heart."

Laura looks at me out of the corner of her eye to see if I am looking at her with disapproval for her flippancy. I am.

"Well, excuse me, but I have trouble getting down to being very serious. Being a good young girl of the old South I was raised to be silly. Serious is hard work.

"OK, the trouble is I still think about Dave and all we had together for that year. It was truly, truly magical. Now, Charlie is wonderful too—but not really magical. Do any of you understand me?"

"Dave made your toes curl, maybe," offers Sophie.

"Exactly! But not just in bed. When he talked to me about any-thing—anything at all—I got tingles all down my back. He made me itch."

"Oh, boy, I remember *that* feeling," remarks Patricia.

"Now when I was Ms. Widowlady with my tear-stained cheeks, I never remembered any of that because I was mad at him for dying. It didn't start until after I married Charlie. Then all of a sudden there's Dave in my head messing with my emotions and making me feel guilty about Charlie. Would you believe that I've actually considered divorc-ing Charlie because I now feel like I'm cheating on both of them? It's crazy but that's what it feels like."

"Have you told Charlie about all this?" I ask.

"Are you crazy? Of course not. Now there's a thought. 'Charlie, darlin', I have something to tell you. I'm cheatin' on you with my dead husband.'"

"Well, Dave knows about Charlie, doesn't he?"

"What?"

"In your mind, Laura, does Dave know about Charlie?"

"Well, I guess so. Yes, in fact I remember asking him what he thought about all this. Crazy as *that* sounds. So, yes, Dave knows about Charlie."

"What does he say about it?"

"Oh, my God, must I really do this? He approves. I mean he understands and accepts it. Whatever."

"Well, I think Charlie deserves the same opportunity that you gave Dave. Laura, you want to make a life with this man and you're thinking of leaving him because you've been remembering your dead husband. That's pretty serious. I think Charlie knows something is wrong. We men may seem dumb and insensitive because we don't notice that you stopped painting your nails Jungle Red, but in matters of feeling we are just as intuitive as you ladies. Trust me on this one. Tell Charlie."

"What if he asks me if I'm thinking about Dave when we make love? Men get very competitive about that."

"You can lie about that."

"You old phony," she shouts and throws a pillow at me.

"Better safe than sorry," I reply. "Seriously, Laura, talk to Charlie about all this. I'm sure he'll understand. You don't want to destroy your marriage because your grieving has taken a comical turn."

"It's not funny."

"Oh, yes it is. Sad and funny and touching. Look at what you've done for yourself. You stopped being angry at Dave for dying and you rediscovered how much you loved him. I'd say that was a good thing. Oh, Laura, you loved Dave and now you know it, you know what a loving woman you are. Go and lavish all that love on Charlie. And don't be too surprised if one day you find your toes curling up again."

Afterglow

The aftermath of death is grief. But what is the aftermath of love? I call it *afterglow*, and anyone who has ever really been in love knows exactly what I mean.

The afterglow of love is more than just a memory, more than a reminiscence. It is a sensory experience that involves sight and sound as well as smell and taste and touch. A memory is like a flashback in which moments from our past play across our inner eye, with or without a soundtrack. A reminiscence is more like the longing of nostalgia and involves feelings about people and places from our past.

But in afterglow we get all the senses. When we love someone, every one of our senses imprints images of them on our brain until we have perfectly recorded them. These memory images are there inside our brain forever, perfectly archived, ready for instant recall. Instant afterglow.

When the one we love dies, we grieve, and grieve, and grieve. During our grieving we retrieve our afterglow to comfort us.

In the darkness, a widow calls her beloved husband to her and once again she feels his touch, hears his voice, and is enveloped in the fragrance of his body. He is *there* with her, just as he was before his death.

Buying a new car, she turns to her husband (in her mind) and asks his opinion. There is no sentimental foolishness here. We always know what someone we love thinks. We always *know*, in our hearts, what they would say or do in a given situation. And in her mind the widow's husband reminds her to ask about the ratio of miles per gallon and what sort of rear suspension the car has.

Later that day, he tells her that the yellow dress she's trying on reminds him of one she wore that summer they went to Paris. She was only 18 then—she is 50 now—but she buys it just the same because she is wrapped in their afterglow.

But comforting as these remembrances can be, they can be dangerous and beguiling too. Dangerous because we can become entrapped by them. Beguiling because they have a magical quality that may deceive us.

Sometimes, memories can hold us prisoner in the past, keeping us from reentering life. And they can make a man who was only 5'10" seem like a giant—a super hero with whom no living man can compete.

As a certified romantic, I encourage every grieving person to enter the realm of the afterglow where they can forever enjoy the presence of the one they love who has died.

The only caution I have is to watch out for the times when the afterglow interferes with making a new life and new memories.

If we constantly rerun the memories of our love in the little corner window of our mental screen we can become distracted from the main event on the big screen of life—the here and now.

Thankfully, our memories cannot be erased or recorded over. When, and if, we love again, our afterglow is always intact. But we can now make a new and different set of memories that, in time, will co-exist with the others.

I often suggest that a widow wrap the warm, wooly comforter of afterglow around herself like a cocoon. And when the time is right, she can shed her cocoon, and she will emerge as a beautiful butterfly.

· ·

Terry

I imagine Terry as one of those girls who is often the subject of concerned aunts. They usually say something like, "That girl is so homely she'll never get a man." And if she does get married they predict her children will all be "homely as sin." What's interesting to me is that most really beautiful women were homely little girls.

Looking at Terry now I can see that what is wonderful about her face and figure could only be the result of having once been a homely child. Her hair is the color of freshly cut wheat and her huge brown eyes dominate her face. Her lips are full and sensuous, but a child with that mouth was probably called something awful like "fish-face." She was never the high-school prom queen, but by the time she left college and came to New York, she was good looking enough to turn heads on any street. She got a job in advertising, eventually became a creative director, and married one of the clients. One of the richer ones. When he was killed in a plane crash, she thought her life was over.

"When Lee was killed I thought about suicide right away. I was never a very happy child and even after I came to New York and enjoyed a bit of success, I wasn't really happy. Then I met Lee, and for the first time in my life I thought I was happy. Not fairy tale, Prince Charming happy, but deep down warm and cozy happy. Men are so funny about romance. They always make it so elaborate. Most girls just want to feel safe and comfortable with a man. Oh, I know plenty about sexy, dangerous men, but women who go for that type just haven't figured things out yet. Sooner or later they wise up and start looking around for someone cozy.

"Lee was ripe and ready when he met me, and I just let him discover how wonderful I was all by himself. I was always easygoing and friendly, but just a little bit mysterious. I'd been selling products for five years and I knew a thing or two about marketing. My boss used to rant on and on about targeting your market, so when I spotted Lee I mentally put a bull's-eye on his back and went to work on my campaign. Fourteen months later we were married and intending to live happily ever after. You hear a lot of talk about love and what it is and how to get it and all that stuff, but the truth is that if you think about the man you love as a rare and precious possession, it's easy to know what to do about it. So I treated him like my own special Ming vase. I put him on a pedestal and didn't let him get dusty. And he treated me exactly the same way.

"I wish I could say that after he was killed that I cried my heart out and was totally and completely devastated, but that isn't what happened at all. Oh, I cried all right and I was mad as hell, and I drank and smoked too much, and I gained weight, and looked awful, but I wasn't shattered. I stayed in one piece. I was just a little mussed up. Take note that I didn't say *messed* up.

"I looked around and realized that as long as I stayed in New York, I'd be haunted by his memory—so I packed up and moved to San Francisco.

"So there I was in the city by the bay, and all I could do was point out the sights to Lee. That's right, folks, he came right along for the ride. Oh, the other lovely thing about San Francisco was that I saw him everywhere. Well, we all know about that little number. So, I moved to Dallas and it was the same thing all over again. The good thing was, I stopped seeing him because they don't have men like Lee in Texas. But he was still in my head and I was still dreaming about him at night, and I would get really lonesome, have a few martinis, and settle down for a good cry.

"I've been sitting here listening to women talk about their husbands and their grief and sometimes I think I'm not doing it right.

Sometimes I think that one of the side effects of loving Lee and his loving me, is that I don't remember how to be really unhappy.

"Where was I? Oh, after Dallas came Aspen, and then Philadelphia. Then I decided that it was all a foolish waste of time and I moved back to New York. At least in New York I didn't take Lee sightseeing in my head. I went back to work at another agency, and maybe some day I'll find another eligible client.

"Sometimes I look in the mirror at myself and I say, 'Look at you, a man really loved you, isn't that wonderful.' And then I say, 'Yeah, ain't life grand!'

"I'm a lucky woman and I know it. I never expected life would be this good. I know I'll always be a widow, but I'm determined to be a merry one."

Home

I was a very young boy the first time I saw Dorothy click the heels of her ruby red slippers together and intone the magical phrase, "There's no place like home, there's no place like home." At the time, it seemed the perfect ending to a wonderful adventure, a trip to the Land of Oz and then home to Kansas and Auntie Em.

Unfortunately, home isn't always a safe haven, and I'm sure that there are battered women and children who would rather have stayed in Oz. They might be joined there by a group of widows who no longer find home to be where the heart is. Death puts a chill on everything, even what was once a warm and cozy hearth.

Depending on a number of factors, like age and money, a new widow often chooses to move away from her home, and to start over. Once filled with the sounds of children and a laughing husband, her home may now be too empty, or too expensive to maintain. Very often, the house has too many memories, and the sadness the memories invoke is more than some women can endure. So they move away, seeking a new beginning.

The place we call home is generally thought to be a safe place, but when a woman becomes a widow, home can feel like a nightmare, or like a prison in which she is trapped. Suddenly, her dream house becomes haunted, and she struggles to escape the thousand tiny, every-day memories that make her life a living hell.

In time, many of the nightmares will fade, and the memories that caused heartache will bring comfort and joy. But that may take many months, even years, and a widow needs answers immediately.

Depending on age and financial status, a widow may choose to keep her home, even though it is filled with painful memories. So she might need to travel for a while as part of her grieving process. Or she may let her children take over the family home, if they want it. She might even rent it for a year or two until she feels comfortable with the idea of living there alone.

Whatever she decides to do, her action should not be taken in the heat of the moment. If love is blind, grief is blinding, and no decisions as important as where to make her home should be made in haste.

They say that home is where the heart is, and I believe that's true. Home is a physical place. Home is a psychological place. And home is a spiritual place.

And memories can be home too. Memories are like money in the bank. They grow in value over time, and we can draw them out, like cash, whenever we need or want to. So long after the physical home is gone, the spiritual and psychological home remain within our hearts and minds.

In time, when a widow becomes a solitaire, she too can sing the words of that old song—"anywhere I hang my hat is home."

· ·

Rachel

The afternoon light had faded and turned into golden twilight as the day became evening. I lit the fire in the fireplace, refilled my coffee cup, and wondered if Rachel was going to talk to us today.

She had been a widow for less than a year and her grief was so intense, so devastating, that she seldom got out of bed before noon and rarely left the house unless it was really necessary.

Rachel joined us after her doctor introduced us. She was heavily sedated and he feared that she'd become dependent on drugs. Nothing seemed to lift her depression, and when I explained what our group did she simply shrugged and agreed to come.

Week after week she came but never said a word, never talked about herself, never commented on what others said. After a while she reluctantly joined the chain but always placed herself last. She insisted that she had made no progress and I agreed with her.

I watched her now as she sat apart from the group, holding her cup in both hands as if warming herself. She must have been pretty once, perhaps even beautiful, but now she looked drawn and haggard, all of life sapped out of her. We'd talked a couple of times by ourselves. Actually, I did the talking, she sat looking at me as though I were some stranger from another world speaking a language she neither knew nor understood.

In every sense of the word, Rachel was the epitome of grief and despair. It was literally carved in her face like giant, ugly scars.

Just before we'd taken another break, we'd started talking about honoring and remembering. Sophie was talking about her beloved Avram and how much she cherished the memories of their early married days. Now, she picked up where she left off.

"So, my darling Avram took the horse . . ."

"Stop it! Stop it!" Rachel suddenly screamed. "Stop talking about remembering. I hate that!" She pulled at her sweater and clenched her hands into reddened fists. She was pacing around the circle, staring wildly into our faces as if to find one face that understood, that would confirm her emotions.

"What is the matter with all of you? Are you all crazy? How can you talk about remembering? Where the hell is your pain?" She stopped in front of me, her fingers clenched and unclenched, spread wide apart in frustration. "Don't you get it? I don't want memories— I want my husband!"

She was right, of course. No one wants a memory. A memory is a poor substitute for the real thing. A memory can't hold you in its arms or fill you with pleasure. A memory can't tease you or make you laugh or surprise you with roses on your birthday. In a world where the living are gleaming, glistening diamonds, a memory is a lackluster imitation of the real thing.

"You can all take your memories and . . ." She turned around facing each of us, indicting us with her eyes. Then she sat down, hands folded primly in her lap, waiting for us to respond. I wondered who would answer her, who could answer her. I hoped the task wouldn't fall to me.

Out of the corner of my eye I saw Patricia smooth her skirt and speak.

"For weeks now, Rachel, you've assigned yourself the last link in our chain and we allowed you. We let you because all of us have been there and don't really want to admit that we're moving ahead—making progress. Moving ahead seems like forgetting. And forgetting is a sin, an infidelity. Moving ahead feels like you've stopped caring and stopped loving.

"So we sat by and let you stay there for your own good and your own comfort because we *all* understand.

"But tonight, dear friend, you have moved forward with lightning speed and brought all of us with you. You have said the words we all fear to say and hate to hear. You have torn open all the old wounds we thought were healing. Rachel, dear Rachel, your rage, your fury, gives meaning to your love and to ours."

She reached out her hand to Rachel. "Not one of us wants to settle for anything less than the real thing, but the truth is this: your beloved husband is dead. The real thing is gone. Margarine isn't the real thing. Butter is. But if there is no butter, if the butter is gone, then you must make do with the next best thing.

"I don't want my life to be dry toast. I want it covered in rich golden butter. But my butter is gone, and all I have left is the memory of its richness, its pure golden color, and its sweet taste. The margarine of memory can never, ever, replace or even approximate the real thing. But, Rachel, it is better than a life of dry toast!

"Stewart is dead, Rachel, dead and buried and gone. Forever. Your butter is gone, just like mine is gone, and every other woman's in this room is gone. Yes, we all spread our lives with the margarine of memory—we have no choice about that. But all you have to do— all you *can* do now—is decide if you want the rest of your life to be dry toast. Think about that."

In silence we all thought about a life of dry toast. And we all thought about the rich golden butter that once enriched and nourished us. It was the dismal prospect of a life of dry toast that had brought these women together in the first place. Here, in Harmony, they share their recipes for life, using margarine.

As night closed around us we stood holding hands in a circle. This is the moment we speak our secret word of memory and I asked Rachel to begin.

"Butter," she intoned.

"Butter," said Margaret.

"Butter," said Helen.

"Butter," said Sophie.

"Butter," said Marie.

"Butter," said Joan.

"Butter," said Lisa.

"Butter," said Patricia.

"Butter," said Laura.

"Butter," said Terry.

"Butter," I said, completing the circle.

Rage

Shortly after my book *After Goodbye* was published, I received a letter from a young girl thanking me for giving her permission to grieve as long as she needed and wanted. She had read several other books that seemed to be saying what her family and friends were telling her. Stop grieving. Get on with your life. Those words were like a knife in her heart.

Only someone who has never experienced the death of someone they dearly loved would suggest that there is any possible way to stop grieving. That loss is with us forever, and so is the grief. It just changes as time goes by. In time it changes from a sharp pain to a dull pain, but it remains a pain we carry with us always.

If a widow is left confused about who she is after the death of her beloved husband, she is even more confused by her feelings of anger—her pure rage—at his dying and leaving her alone. Rage simply isn't *nice*.

Rage is exactly the same thing as grief. Rage is the companion of loss. No matter how we express it or try to explain it, the simple truth is we are angry about our loss. We grieve for *who* is gone. We rage for *what* is gone.

"I weep because Tom is dead. I'm angry because my husband is gone."

Rage and grief cut deeply into our hearts and minds. In time, the pain will subside but never completely stop. The wounds will heal but there will be a scar. In time, even the scar will fade and become almost invisible. Only you will know where it is.

If these wounds don't seem to be healing, get help. Deep wounds often need helping hands and a long time to heal.

Fortunately, society has become more accepting of the rage in all of us who have suffered the loss of a loved one. We no longer need a stiff upper lip. We can kick and scream and shed all the tears we want without too much disapproval.

But don't put a cork in it. Don't keep it bottled up. Stand in your living room and scream your lungs out. And if you need to, fling open your window and shout those immortal words, "I'm mad as hell, and I'm not going to take it anymore."

Then shut the window and do something about it.

Reunion

A little more than a year has passed since the ten women gathered in this room to talk about what being a widow meant to them. I guess we're all a little wiser, I know we're all a little older. All of us, except Sophie.

Not all of them made it back in person, but those that didn't have kept me posted on their search for solitaire.

None of us is surprised to learn that Sophie remarried. Sooner or later, all that shuffleboard had to pay off. She's living in Bermuda now and sends me letters and postcards regularly. A few weeks before the wedding, these words arrived from her:

"Darling Mister Bear, I may not be a solitaire yet but I just got one for my finger that would knock your socks off. This boy has a real eye for gems—he got me, didn't he? Believe me, I had a lot of offers but I decided that I should marry a younger man who can bury me. I don't think I could stand to be a widow again. Trust me, he's a wonderful boy and he takes real good care of me and I take real good care of him. Tell Terry I remember what she said about the Ming vase, she's absolutely right. I keep my darling so busy he has no time to get dusty.

Love to everyone from Sophie who is *still* a very Jewish woman."

Also not with us is Helen who died a month ago. A few weeks after we had all gathered together for the last time, she was diagnosed with cancer. She waged a terrific battle and never once complained about her pain or suffering. A few days after she found out about her cancer she came to see me. She'd bought a red dress and red shoes and the most delightful hat I'd ever seen. In that outfit she was the most beautiful ruby-red solitaire I have ever seen. I'm sure that God will be pleased to have one bright red angel in His heavenly choir.

And Rachel committed suicide. A life without butter was more than she could handle.

"Well, Laura," I ask, "how is married life these days?"

"Couldn't be better. Of course, being married to two men at the same time is a bit of a chore. Just kidding. I finally got up the nerve to tell Charlie about Dave and he was just adorable about it. He knew all about it anyway. It seems that I talk in my sleep and a couple of times I slipped and called him Dave while we were, you know, being sexy.

"It has gotten to be a sort of family joke. Every now and then he says that he's been talking things over with Dave and they've decided such and such. Sometimes I laugh and sometimes I get angry because I thought he was making fun of me.

"I know that I can't qualify as a solitaire because I'm married again, but a part of me found the thing inside me that I think you're talking about. The only way I can describe it is to say that if Charlie died tomorrow I'd be OK. Part of me believes he'd be OK too, because Dave would look out for him. But more important than that is my own understanding of myself as a woman. That's who I am. A woman. Sure, I'm a wife and a widow, but those are secondary descriptions of *what* I am. A woman is *who* I am and I define that for myself. Gemstones are created by the earth pressing down on them. They are created by the pressures around them. And their beauty is a result of that experience. If they are weak, they shatter. If they are resilient and strong, they become gemstones. And in that sense, I am a solitaire.

"And one more thing. Dave taught Charlie how to curl my toes."

"How are you doing, Patricia?" I ask, already knowing the answer.

"Well, I ended up marrying a client and Mister Bear gave me away. Frankly, I think he was glad to get rid of me.

"I think, like Laura, I found my solitaire and that let me let go of everything painful about my grief. And I was lucky because I met a man who understood everything because his wife had died five years earlier leaving him with a young daughter to raise. I think we knew right away that we were going to fall in love but I know he was as scared of it as I was. But we were lucky because we had had good partners the first time and so we expected to be happy. Thankfully, his daughter was old enough to be friends with me and I didn't have to deal with being her new mother, just her new best buddy. And I agree with Laura that if, God forbid, I had to do it again, I could. But if you want to meet a real solitaire you should talk to Terry."

"OK, Patty, lay off," responds Terry, who looks more beautiful than ever. "I'm still single and not looking to change that anytime soon. I date occasionally, but nothing you'd call serious. But I'm not an all-work-and-no-play lady either. I think I'm a kind of one-man woman. Sophie used to say that, but she meant one at a time. I guess all this talk about going solo and being a solitaire really got to me. After Lee died and I kept running from city to city trying to escape my grief, I finally realized that it was going to be with me forever. You never stop grieving—it just changes. The pain reminds you how good it was, and you remember that a man really, really loved you and it made you feel wonderful. I don't know if I even want to try that again. Knowing that made me want to find out more about the woman that man loved—me. I needed to know so I could love me too. After months and months of pulling myself along that damn widow's chain I finally saw that I was at the top link. I had found myself, knew who I was, and felt good about it. When Lee died I thought that part of me had died but then I began to understand that I was still intact and that all of him was still with me and he would be as long as I lived. And that nourishes and enriches me beyond anything else. It puts a smile on my face."

I look over at Lisa who looks as fresh as a house with a new coat of paint.

"Your turn at bat, Lisa," I say with a smile.

"I really wish that Sophie was here so I could thank her. After all those months of her nagging me to do something with myself, I finally did. It turns out I have a real knack for computers. Shortly after I went to work for one company, another one tried to recruit me—sight unseen. And that's where the trouble started. I went for the interview and didn't get the job. I know it was because I looked like a moth-eaten widow woman instead of the person they thought I was.

"So, I joined a health club, lost weight, bought some new clothes, and went back to work hoping that I might get another chance. Funny thought. That's what this is really all about—a second chance at life. Anyway, as luck would have it, I ran into the guy who interviewed me at a computer programmers' seminar. He didn't even recognize me at first, and when he did figure out who I was, he offered me a job right then and there. And I took it. We celebrated over dinner. That was my first date with a man since I got married and I enjoyed myself.

"I was still a little girl when I got married. Young and cute and eager to please. Who could resist me? So I got married to Joe and it wasn't all bad.

"But I'm a woman now, and I'm enjoying what that means. I see Peggy doing all the stuff I did at her age and I wince—but I hold my tongue because she's got to find her own way. Just like I did then, and like I am now.

"When I got a big promotion last month I went out and bought myself a diamond solitaire ring. It's my graduation present to myself."

"OK, Maggie, your turn."

"Sometimes I long for the old days when I'd think I saw Jack on the street, and he'd touch me under the covers and I'd hear him walking around in the living room. But I know I'm better off now that that doesn't happen any more. But I still miss him and I still think about him and I still wear his favorite perfume. It is never easy to lose someone you love. I've read the books. I've been to support groups. I've dragged myself along the widow's chain and if I've found solitaire I don't know it. I am going solo and I do it pretty well, but I still think of myself as a woman alone, without her husband, and I'm unhappy to be that woman. I think I always will be. But, strangely, it doesn't make me angry to be that woman. I accept that woman and I like and admire her. I couldn't say that a year ago, so I'm making progress.

"I think a lot of women will only have one really good man in their lives. I believe that a few get lucky and find another one, but I think it's a mistake to go looking. A good man is a gift.

"And life is a gift. And love is a gift. And so is happiness. But I believe that of all of them, happiness is the only gift you can give yourself."

"Let's take a coffee break and stretch our arms and legs," I say. "Marie has quite a story to tell and I think a nice hot cup of tea will put us in the mood." Marie and I exchange a smile and I put a couple of extra cookies on my plate to celebrate. I only allow myself sweets on very special occasions. We settle back down and Marie takes a breath and tells her story.

"Some things get worse before they get better. Like a fever before it breaks and you know you'll be OK. After the trip to Washington, I became more and more depressed. That changed slowly into a consuming rage that exploded everywhere. Every time I opened my mouth it was like a bomb going off. Everyone got hit. Finally, the doctor put me on tranquilizers and I quieted down. Then I became dependent on them and had to go to rehab. That was a chilling experience, I'll tell you.

"In rehab we had encounter groups. I thought they'd be like this, nice and civilized. Wrong. They were hell on wheels. I heard language and used language that would make you all blush. We lashed out at each other like animals and some nights I thought I'd die. This was no Betty Ford thing that nice rich people go to when they have a drinking problem. This was a center for 'Nam vets and their families. At first I was the only woman in my group, and they spotted my bad attitude right away. And they nailed me for it.

"I thought when I broke down that morning in Washington that I had had some kind of breakthrough, but it was only the tip of the iceberg. After three weeks in rehab I became an outpatient and went home. I had to attend weekly 12-step meetings and I hated that. So I went back for three more weeks.

"When I came out that time I was a totally different person.

When those boys finished with me I knew myself better than I ever had and I knew what I wanted to do with my life. Now I work five days a week as a therapist in a VA hospital. At night I run widows' groups based on what I've learned here and what I learned in rehab.

"I work with severely handicapped guys who have had parts of their bodies blown away. I help them get used to their artificial arms and legs. I've even taught a few to dance.

"And I have a beautiful man in my life. His name is Tim and he served in the same area that Mark did. He told me everything he could remember until I could see it in my mind and I could see where Mark died.

"I'm not sure that Timmy will ever leave the hospital or even how long he'll live. Most of his lower body was blown away by a land mine. I don't know what you'd call what we feel for one another. Love seems too easy. It's much more complicated than that. These guys are unbelievable, so beautiful in their hearts and souls, so pure. But they have this real dark side too. They make jokes about their pain and suffering. It takes getting used to. Last week he asked me to marry him. You know what he said? He said, 'Honey, how'd you like to be a widow again real soon?'

"'I'm ready,' I said."

I was watching Joan the whole time Marie was talking, and I watched as she smiled and cried as Marie spoke. In this labyrinth we call grief sometimes the way out is through the enemy camp.

"Your turn, Joan," I said smiling. We have become close friends in these long months, and I find myself in the role of baby sitter at least twice a week.

"I know you're all wondering, so I'll get it out of the way first thing. The children and I are still HIV negative. It doesn't mean we're out of the woods, but I think we'll be OK.

"After we got back from seeing the Quilt I felt that some things were resolved—but I also felt that something was missing and I couldn't figure out what. I kept thinking about Jerry, the young man who had been in the hospital with Kenny. I got his address from one of the nurses and I wrote and invited him to come over for lunch. He accepted.

"Lucky for me he suspected why I had invited him and he talked to me for hours about Kenny and then about himself. I won't pretend that I understood all of it, and part of me still hated that part of Kenny that caused his death and jeopardized his family. But I had taken the first step and Jerry was willing to help me. He said there were some guys he wanted me to meet and I agreed to have dinner with them the following week.

"I didn't know what to expect when we joined the group in what was clearly a gay restaurant. There I was, surrounded by nine really good-looking men who were all smiling at me like I was a movie star. For one horrible moment I thought these might all be Kenny's boyfriends. Let me tell you, that idea really made me need a drink.

"But it turned out to be something very different. All of these guys belonged to a group called The Gay Father's Forum which is one of the largest groups in the country. Some of them knew they were gay (or bisexual) when they married and some discovered themselves afterwards. It was amazing and very educational. By the end of the evening I felt as though I'd known them for years, and we were friends. They all said they felt the same way and hoped we could all meet again soon. That night I felt as though I understood Kenny better than I ever had, and I felt that I knew myself better too. The most interesting thing was that I understood that I was attracted to these men. They all had the same energy and quick wit that Kenny had and they knew how to make me feel special and comfortable. I had been driving myself crazy asking why I hadn't seen that Kenny was gay, but now I realized that without realizing it, I had. That aspect of him delighted me. I just didn't know what it was.

"During the week one of the guys called and asked if I'd like to come to a party and bring my kids. I hesitated but he assured me that I wouldn't be the only woman at the party. I went, but I didn't bring my children. I still wasn't sure of what was going on.

"I went to the party and met their wives and children. It felt very strange knowing what I knew—or thought I knew. I felt guilty about not bringing my children but everyone was very nice and didn't say a word about it.

"Listen to me rattle on. Anyway, it helped me to understand that

I wasn't the only woman who got herself into my situation, and that maybe I could have a few friends that I didn't have to be afraid would find out about Kenny and how he died.

"During the next few weeks I really got excited about doing something useful. I was in a unique position and I wanted to do something useful with what I knew.

"I realized that I couldn't possibly be the only wife whose husband had died of AIDS. So I talked to Jerry and I talked to some of the wives and, of course, I talked to Mister Bear. Now we have a Harmony-type group for widows of men who died of AIDS. Not all of these men were gay or bisexual. Many of them were IV drug users. Some of the widows and their children are HIV positive. Sadly, it's a group that gets bigger everyday.

"So, look at me. Am I a solitaire, or what!"

QUESTIONS AND ANSWERS
OVER COFFEE AND CAKE

....

Questions and Answers Over Coffee and Cake

Like the seasons, the widows of Harmony come and go. Some take much longer than others to work up the widow's chain, and in that process, they often need some additional time to talk out certain aspects of their search for solitaire.

Usually, after the Harmony session has come to a close and most of the group has headed home, a few remain behind—for another cup of coffee and to continue the discussion.

And sometimes they stay behind because they aren't ready, or willing, to go back to that empty house.

So we put on a fresh pot of coffee, gather around the kitchen table, and nibble at the remains of the cake.

These women, like the ten we just met, also have a wide range of responses to the strange and unfamiliar situation they now find themselves in.

Karen, whose husband Steve died a few months ago, picks up the discussion.

"I'm really beginning to feel *alone*. After Steve died, I was surrounded by friends and family all the time. There was so much to do, and despite my best efforts, I hardly had a moment to myself. I guess everyone wanted to be helpful and offer their support and comfort, but I felt smothered by it. I tried to look calm on the outside, but inside I was ready to explode. Now that everyone has gone back home I feel relieved. I can finally start to sort things out."

"And how is that going?" I ask.

"Confusing. There seem to be a thousand things to do and, despite my best intentions, I don't seem to be able to do any of them. I make lists but that doesn't help at all. It makes me feel even worse when nothing gets checked off."

"Maybe you should try standing still and doing nothing at all," I suggest. "Maybe you need to take a long, quiet walk in your new shoes. Give yourself a chance to 'break in' this new way of walking."

"You mean my first steps going solo?"

"Partly that, but partly just walking around by yourself, listening to yourself think. We need that kind of time to ourselves. It's like that expression, 'You're talking so much, I can't hear myself think.' By becoming still, we can hear our inner voice. Stillness allows us to simply cry and simply breathe and simply live."

"When Aaron died," says Brenda, "I felt so cheated. I turned myself into an *A-number-one* victim of circumstances. Boy, did that make me unpopular with everyone. I guess I wasn't supposed to complain that I felt shortchanged."

"That isn't *nice*," I remark with a smile.

"No siree, it isn't. I wasn't playing by the rules. I wasn't the poor, pitiful widow sitting in the corner, weeping in her stew. I was a raging bitch. I was shaking my fists at God and death and anyone that suggested that while it wasn't fair, it was the way it was and that was that."

"Aren't we humans a funny bunch," I laughed. "We lose a ball game and it's OK to curse and swear that we were cheated. We lose our jobs and we rant and rave that it isn't fair and no one disagrees. But if we even suggest that death isn't fair, that death cheated us, then society clucks its tongue and turns away."

"We make them uncomfortable," remarks Brenda. "After the funeral we're supposed to shut up and mourn and after a few months we're supposed to get over that and go find another husband."

"You still sound angry, Brenda," I comment. "I thought you said you had that under control."

"Just when I think I do, it comes right back. The other day some guy from an investment firm called about putting my inheritance into bonds and I realized the bastard must be reading death notices to build his client list. I screamed at him so loud I must have broken his eardrum. I slammed the phone down and just let myself cry."

"What were you so angry about?" I ask, already knowing.

"I was angry about being a damn widow!"

One Lump, or Two?

The death of your partner feels like being hit by a speeding car. The force of the impact can hurl you up in the air, and then drop you crashing to the ground, where you sustain multiple injuries. I think most widows would agree that's what it feels like.

Only after weeks in the hospital, your bones mending, your cuts healing, and your bruises fading, do you even consider trying to walk again—possibly with crutches or a cane.

"Well, I did something really dumb last week," says Wendy, smiling and shaking her head.

"Even now, after nearly a year, I still get hit by it at the oddest times. I mean, I think I'm doing fine and then, BAM, and I'm knocked for a loop."

"What happened?" I ask.

"I went to dinner with this really nice guy from my office. Nothing romantic, just an evening out with a man and it felt really good. He knows what I've been through and he's been really great about covering for me when I'd get the blubbers now and then. So, I thought dinner would be nice. Everything was really pleasant until the coffee came and as he reached for the sugar he looked at me and asked, 'One lump, or two?' and it hit me that this really great guy didn't *know* me and I felt horribly, horribly alone."

"Maybe," offers Bonnie, "you were feeling something else."

"What?"

"The starting-over shakes. It seems like after Jack died that everyone was pushing me to get back into the swing of things. I didn't want to really, but I thought maybe I'd feel better if I tried it. So I thought, 'What the hell? I'll go down to the country club and see some friends.' I got dressed up, put on some makeup, and tried not to look like a miserable widow lady.

"Well, I was feeling pretty good about taking my first steps back into the outside world, and when I sat down at the bar and ordered a drink I was actually having some happy memories. The bartender has known me for years, and he greeted me with a smile. But when I ordered my usual drink, he asked if I'd please sit at one of the tables so he could serve me. I said I'd rather sit at the bar, and he got real nervous and then he said, 'I'm sorry, Mrs. Williamson, but we aren't permitted to serve single women at the bar—it's club policy.' I just stared at him, and then I started to laugh hysterically. I left the bar and laughed all the way to my car. Then I sat behind the wheel and cried my heart out."

"What hurts the most," says Vivian as she puts down her coffee cup, "is the little stuff. You expect the big changes in your life and dealing with them isn't all that bad. But the little things, the everyday things, drive you nuts. Stuff like shopping for one and setting the table for one. Suddenly, there's hardly enough dirty laundry for a full load and you start to miss having to put down the toilet seat."

"So, tell us, Mister Bear, what's a widow woman supposed to do?"

"Uh, oh, a pop quiz," I respond with raised eyebrows. "I'd better get into my advisor mode. Well, you asked for it. I think I'll use a little macho imagery. When a car has been in the garage unused for a couple of months, we 'warm it up' by letting the engine *idle*. The engine is turned on and functioning, but it isn't doing any work. Idling the engine of your life is the standing-still part of grieving.

"Sooner or later, most widows reenter the mainstream of life. The timing is unimportant, that's your choice. Just as we are all entitled to grieve as long as we choose, we are entitled to decide when we want to reenter life as a solo person.

"So don't let friends and family, however well-intentioned, push you ahead of your own heart's judgment. You, and only you, know when the time is right to shift into gear."

Love, Honor, and OK

A few months ago, Kathy, one of the widows in my group, asked if I would consider giving her daughter away at her birthday party. It seemed that her daughter, Wendy, wanted a wedding as a birthday present.

The only hitch was that she was six years old.

"Who's the lucky groom?" I inquired.

"An extremely eligible teddy bear," Kathy replied, smiling.

"Well, in that case, I would consider it an honor."

The minister was Wendy's seven-year-old brother, Harris, who seemed unusually delighted to be all dressed up. Perhaps he thought the eligible teddy bear intended to whisk his sister away on a honeymoon, leaving all her toys behind for him.

The ceremony was beautiful and at one point during the vows, Harris sternly asked the bride if she consented to "love, honor, and OK" her husband the bear.

Delighted giggles rippled through the crowd.

When we truly love someone who dies, they live on forever in our hearts. But what happens if we love again? And marry again?

Does that mean we have forgotten? No. Does it mean that we are dishonoring the memory of our loved one who has died? No. Emphatically, NO!

All it means is that we have room in our hearts for a new love. It means that we are beginning again and starting a new history with a new partner.

Later that evening, after all the wedding cake had been eaten, and the newlyweds safely tucked into bed, the "mother of the bride" and the "bridesmaids"—other widows from our Harmony group—joined me once again for coffee and conversation in Kathy's living room.

"It was a very lovely wedding," remarked Susan with a smile. "I even got a little teary."

"You got *very* teary," said Victoria with a laugh.

"Well, I'm just an old softie."

"I especially liked the vows," I said. "Especially the part about 'love, honor, and OK.' I thought it was very profound."

"Profound?" asked Kathy.

"Well, yes. Think how often we've discussed remarriage. Think how many times the topic has turned to whether or not your husband would have approved."

"Is this another one of your word games, Mister Bear?"

"Yes, I confess it is. But think about it for a minute. Wouldn't that have been a wonderful promise to include in your vows? Personally, I like 'OK' a lot more than 'obey.'"

"I'll second that," said Susan. "I'm in the first stages of considering remarriage to a wonderful man named Josh, and I'm still asking Walt for permission and understanding. Yeah, I'd like his vow of OK. I'd like it a lot."

. . . .

Today, with the stigma of remarriage almost entirely gone, a widow can choose to remarry anytime she wants to. Her family and her children might object, but it is still her choice because it is *her* life.

Time and again I have heard a widow say that her husband would have approved. Whether this is true or just wishful thinking I can't say, but it's a healthy attitude either way. Loving, remembering, and honoring come in many forms.

Several months later, Susan did marry Josh. Soon after the wedding, her seven-year-old son asked her if Josh was his new daddy.

"No, Bobby," she answered gently. "Josh is my new husband—and I hope he'll be your new friend."

Second-Hand Rose

"I could describe my life in song titles," Sophie once said. "Like 'Second-Hand Rose.'"

"Right now, darlings, I'm humming 'Love Is Lovelier the Second Time Around'—only my darling daughter doesn't approve. And her just back from a Vegas divorce. Talk about glass houses. I took her with me on a cruise, and every time I flirted with a fella she'd get all uptight and say, 'Mother, please, behave yourself.' Listen to her!"

"Sounds like role reversal to me," I commented.

"Maybe sour grapes if you ask me. I got more fellas."

"Sophie, you're a role model to us all," I replied.

"You're kidding me."

"A little bit," I smiled. "But you do present a formidable example of getting back into the swing of things."

"Anyone else have trouble with their kids?" I ask.

Everyone laughs and starts talking at once. Children present a special problem when a widow considers remarriage. It is hardly ever a smooth transition for her children, even when they are grown up and married themselves. Actually, young kids are a lot better behaved about Mommy getting remarried than a lot of grown kids are.

"It's all the little things that crop up. Should I put all my husband's photographs away when my new Prince Charming comes to call? Should I also hide the kids?" says Patty.

"How about that old comparison or competition thing that crops up?" asks Marion. "When it happens in my head I understand it, but the kids? I invited Tom over for Thanksgiving and all hell broke loose. My kids carried on until I finally apologized and asked Tom not to come." She shakes her head. "Kids."

A man who marries a widow with children should realize what he's taking on. I'm sure that anything that helps to make the situation work will be acceptable to him, even welcome, so when the special events and holidays roll around, I suggest that a few moments of remembrance and honoring are very much in order. A graduation card that says: "Your father would be so proud of you today," and signed by both the mother and her new husband, would go a long way towards letting her child know that his father has not been forgotten.

"Thanksgiving was rough on us the first year after I married Bob," said Barbara. "Terry and Charlie, Jr. were eight and ten and understood everything, but they were still difficult at times—especially during the holidays which were always very special times for us. When I served the turkey, I said, 'Charles always carved the turkey for us. He knew just how to get the slices perfectly even. How about it, Bob, do you want to try your hand at it?' I think that helped."

With that simple request, Barbara honored her husband's memory. She let her children see that honoring, and share in the memory. And, by including Bob in that honoring, she helped her children accept her new husband.

First love is always that—*first* love, never forgotten. But a second-hand rose has a fragrance all its own.

· ·

Heads or Tails

Memories can be both painful and pleasurable. Like the other emotional coins in our pocket, memory is two-sided, each side bearing equal value.

Remembering a loved one who has died can plunge us into a pit of depression one minute and send us off into gales of laughter the next. One moment it's tears of sorrow, and the next it's tears of joy. Heads or tails—you take your chances.

But no memory is so painful that it cannot produce, at certain moments, a feeling of pleasure. And no memory of pleasure is without the ability to cause sadness. The best example of this is childbirth. Any mother will tell you that the pain and pleasure aspects of *that* memory coin were fully functional when that event took place.

Victoria invited me to visit her at the shore. The sun warmed our backs as we strolled along the water's edge, and even in late September the sand was warm between my toes.

"You're lucky to have this beautiful beach as your front yard," I remarked with genuine envy.

"Yes, I am. It was a lifesaver after Jeffrey died. I could drive out here and hide out. Just me and my memories."

"Good company."

"Sometimes, but not always. We fought a lot, you know. I look back at those arguments, and I regret them so much."

"Did you kiss and make up afterwards?" I asked.

"Of course."

"Think about that instead. Besides, having a difference of opinion is what makes the world go 'round. It would be awfully boring if everyone agreed all the time."

"I hurt him."

"Did he hurt you?"

"No, of course not," she replied defensively.

"Then you probably didn't hurt him. Love is a pretty strong suit of armor."

"Everything seems like yesterday. The day we met. The day he proposed. Our wedding. Our kids."

"His funeral?" I asked gently.

"No, not really. I was so out of it I can hardly remember any of it. That was the most terrible moment of my life and I can't even tell you what anyone said or did."

"I think it's amazing that the same memory can bring both pain and pleasure," I said. "But, it's even more amazing that time, the greatest healer of all, can brighten the colors of happy memories while fading the tones of sad ones. That, in itself, is a blessing."

"Yes, it is," she said softly.

. . . .

Remembering is a tricky business. The coin of memory is like any other. Flip it in the air and you take your chances, heads or tails. Happy or sad. In the end what is most important is that you have that coin—and that is always a blessing.

Epilogue: *"Who I Am."*

People sometimes become annoyed with me because I like to play this little game with them: I believe that the answer to many questions is contained within the question itself. In my first book I used the question "What can I do?" to examine how people deal with approaching death. By rearranging the same words we got the answer, "Do what I can."

Jesse asked the timeless widow's question, "Who am I?" What she was actually asking was "Who am I *now?*" I think Jesse knew herself pretty well, but what she needed to know was how to understand herself as a widow. The quest for solitaire is the search, in part, for that answer.

Several months after that gray afternoon when Jesse posed her question, she called me and asked if we could meet for coffee. During the months that followed that first Harmony session, she had been meeting with the widows and working her way along the chain. I was curious about why she wanted a private session over coffee.

I watched her cross the street and admired her new appearance. She had cut her hair short, which made her features stand out more attractively, and she was dressed in a very pretty dress with a billowing skirt. She looked perky. She entered the coffee shop, spotted me, and eased her way through the tables and collapsed in her chair after kissing me on the cheek.

"You look pretty sassy for a widow woman," I chided.

"Don't start with me, Mister Bear," she wagged a warning finger at me. "This no-nonsense lady means business and I won't stand for any rib poking by the likes of you."

"I'll behave," I replied in a meek voice.

"Not likely but I've got my eye on you. I'm feeling way too good to let you rain on my parade."

"Sounds interesting."

"I just signed the contracts for my new business. The bank is giving us a substantial line of credit, my partner is a dream, and I'm a house afire. And, you old sweetie, I owe it all to you." She smiled and patted my hand.

"I think you overstate my importance but thanks anyway. Why don't you slow down and tell me what *you* did."

"OK. May I have an espresso, please?"

I signaled the waiter, ordered a refill and returned my attention to Jesse.

"Well, let's see. Oh, yes. Well, do you remember my crazy neighbor Beth who got divorced shortly after Brian died? She's the one who dragged me to 'Chippendales'?"

"Kicking and screaming all the way," I remarked dryly.

"Don't be mean. Anyway, Beth just about drove me crazy but she was really a good tonic for my blues and managed to keep me sane for a couple of months. I was doing pretty good with the group, too. I felt myself moving along the chain, and one night I was at the end and out the door on my own. Do you remember the day I kept asking, 'Who am I?' Well, I found the answer just the way you told me to. I turned the question around and got the answer, 'Who I am.' Of course, I didn't exactly know what that meant, but I knew that I had to be who I had to be. I thought about it and talked about it, and then I thought about the thing you said about the original question really being, 'Who am I now?' And when I turned that around it hit me like a bolt of lightning—'Who I am now!'

"Well, that made all the difference to me. I saw myself in the context of the moment. Brian was gone. I was alone. And that was that. So, I stepped back, looked at myself in the moment, decided it wouldn't do, and set about to make a few changes. That's it in a nutshell."

She smiled and sipped her espresso. It sounded good but I wondered what she'd done with her sorrow.

"How do you feel about Brian, now?" I asked.

"I love him more than ever. I even read all his favorite books. It made me feel close to him. I had two of his tweed jackets recut to fit me. It made me feel like he was hugging me. Actually that's how I got the idea for our business."

"You're recutting men's jackets?"

"No, no. We're reselling old bridal gowns. Do you want to know what we call our business?"

"Sure," I replied smiling at her obvious delight.

"Second Time Around."

· · · · · · · · · ·
Resources

There are no easy answers to difficult questions. Each of us must continue to search for exactly the right answers to our specific questions. That search will probably take an entire lifetime, because every answer usually poses another question.

Just as each widow is at a different point along the widow's chain, each of us is at a different point in our grief and our rediscovery.

All around us are signposts and guides that are helpful to us in our quest. From support groups to self-help groups, from open forums to lectures, and to books like this one, many suggestions and answers are offered. Hopefully, you will find the help you are looking for in one or more of these places.

Over the years, the widows have returned again and again to two books as a source of reassurance and confirmation.

First is Lynne Caine's book, *Widow,* published by Bantam Books in 1987. This powerful book resonates with the rage and agony of being left alone. Currently it is only available in libraries.

The second book, also published by Bantam Books, is not a book about the loss of life but the loss of love. In their book, *How to Survive the Loss of a Love,* authors Melba Colgrove, Harold H. Bloomfield, and Peter McWilliams combine short essays with poetry and touch on every aspect of life after the loss of love. It is currently available in libraries and bookstores.

Finally, if you would like to ask a question or share an experience, please feel welcome to write to me, c/o:

The Harmony Project
Box 28K
300 East 40th Street
New York, NY 10016